W9-CLU-496

Praise for *The Celebrity Experience*

"It's said there's not a lot of traffic on the extra mile. Well, *The Celebrity Experience* goes there with its real-world examples and specific suggestions. Cutting's delightful style, blended with her focus on bottom-line results, makes this book a must for anyone who deals with the public."

—Sam Horn, 15-time emcee of the Maui
Writers Conference and author of *POP!*
Stand Out in Any Crowd

"As Donna Cutting highlights in *The Celebrity Experience*, each of us wants to be treated with personalized, compassionate, and just plain special attention. At Country Meadows Retirement Communities, we are preparing to serve the seniors of the future. The celebrity experience is exactly what Baby Boomers will expect from their independent and assisted living providers."

—G. Michael Leader, President and CEO,
Country Meadows Retirement Communities

"*The Celebrity Experience* is rock solid. Not only does Donna Cutting share what any business can do to give red-carpet customer service, the examples and case studies she includes make this practical book interesting, easy to read, and, frankly, fun! Anyone who has a business or a professional practice should buy a copy immediately."

—Susan RoAne, keynote speaker and author
of *How to Work a Room*

"Can everyone please read this book? I want to be treated like a celebrity! Put the person back into personal service and gain clients who love to praise you and pay you. Donna Cutting has written an enlightening, powerful, and fun guide so you can make every client feel like a star!"

—Chellie Campbell, author of *Zero to
Zillionaire* and *The Wealthy Spirit*

The Celebrity Experience

The Celebrity Experience

Insider Secrets to Delivering
Red Carpet Customer Service

Donna Cutting

John Wiley & Sons, Inc.

Published by John Wiley & Sons, Inc., Hoboken, New Jersey.
Published simultaneously in Canada.

Wiley Bicentennial Logo: Richard J. Pacifico

Designations used by companies to distinguish their products are often claimed by trademarks. In all instances where the author or publisher is aware of a claim, the product names appear in Initial Capital letters. Readers, however, should contact the appropriate companies for more complete information regarding trademarks and registration.

For general information on our other products and services or for technical support, please contact our Customer Care Department within the United States at (800) 762-2974, outside the United States at (317) 572-3993 or fax (317) 572-4002.

Wiley also publishes its books in a variety of electronic formats. Some content that appears in print may not be available in electronic books. For more information about Wiley products, visit our web site at www.wiley.com.

Library of Congress Cataloging-in-Publication Data:

Cutting, Donna, 1966–
    The celebrity experience : insider secrets to delivering red carpet customer service / Donna Cutting.
      p. cm.
    ISBN 978-0-470-17401-2 (cloth : acid-free paper)
     1. Customer services. 2. Customer relations. 3. Consumer satisfaction.
    4. Success in business. I. Title.
    HF5415.5.C88   2007
    658.8'12—dc22
                                2007026310

10 9 8 7 6 5 4 3 2 1

To Philip and Patricia Bouchard—Dad and Mom
Thank you for nurturing my creative dreams.

To Jim Cutting—my best friend and husband
You are my favorite adventuring partner and my dream come true.

To Joan Brannick, PhD, Sandy Geroux, David Glickman, and Dave Timmons—my Mastermind Partners
It is my great joy to travel this journey of not-so-impossible dreams with you.

This author is donating a percentage of her royalties to the Second Wind Dreams organization.

Contents

Preface

IMAGINE A WORLD where red carpets were rolled out for you wherever you went, where people greeted you by name, with a smile and boundless enthusiasm. Imagine feeling loved, wanted, and expected everywhere you traveled.

Imagine a life where the people you did business with knew you inside and out and bent over backward to cater to your personal preferences.

Imagine what it would be like if the people around you were so creative and committed to your happiness that they would do almost anything to ensure that all your desires, whims, and wishes were fulfilled.

Imagine . . .

Does such a world exist?

You bet it does. It's called Hollywood. And it's reserved for an elite few.

For the rest of us, however, life plays out a little differently.

We live in a world where we can't get a real person on the phone, we can't find anyone to answer our question, and if we do find someone to help us, we're often told, "That's not my department."

We live in a world where we are sometimes served by people who are so uninterested in us that they are carrying on complete conversations with a coworker while they are engaged (or should I say disengaged?) in our transaction.

We live in a world where we hear "No," or "I don't know," more often than "Yes!"

We live in a world where business is done by computers, we are known by a number instead of a name, we've got to take a number to be waited on, and where we are often made to wait by the same people who won't wait for us. (Try showing up late for your doctor's appointment or your flight.)

If you're like most people, you've dreamed of what it would be like to be treated as a celebrity . . . even if for just a little while. You've dreamed of being expected and warmly welcomed wherever you traveled, of having people cater to your every whim, of having planes held for you, and special tables waiting for you in your favorite restaurants.

Guess what? Your customers are wishing the same thing.

What if you could take the ball in *your* hands and run with it? What if you could give *your* customers the level of service that would make them feel like the most catered-to Hollywood star?

Impossible, you say? Not so, I say!

Honestly, it doesn't take much to make people feel like they are getting the star treatment. Just a firm belief that anything is possible and a commitment to doing what it takes to know your customers inside and out and to delight them in ways that make them say, "Wow!" It takes a yes attitude on the part of everyone on your team, and it takes action!

Before I elaborate, let me tell you a little bit about where I got the idea for *The Celebrity Experience*.

For several years, I worked in the field of elder care with seniors who live in assisted-living communities. If you've ever had to help a parent move into a retirement care community then you know how difficult it can be for everyone. It would break my heart watching children and their parents wrestle with the decision.

The elders themselves are faced with a loss of control, having others make decisions for them, losing their homes, their cars, and everything that once represented their independence. They also face their own mortality, and a move to an assisted-living community feels like giving up.

The adult children are wracked with guilt, often dealing with parents who are fighting the decision, and filled with confusion about whether they are making the right choice.

Despite what you may hear on the news or on the television ads sponsored by law firms, most elder care professionals are sensitive to this transition and bend over backward to be helpful and make it easier. However, as with many industries, they are often short of staff and are overregulated, which sometimes means that people get shortchanged as a result of the process.

Cut to the conversation I had with my friend Andrea, a marketing director at a large assisted-living company. She was telling me about an idea that she and her boss had about how they would welcome prospective and new residents to their community.

At their community, prospective residents and their family members would be welcomed by a valet at the front drive. The valet would be expecting them, and would greet them by name and with a smile as he helped them out of their car.

Another designated greeter would walk the visitors down a red carpet and into the building. Inside they would see a banner that welcomed them personally to the community.

Then they would be escorted immediately to the marketing office. As they made their way down the hallway, they would receive warm smiles and greetings from several people—all of whom seemed to expect them and to be glad they were there.

Upon their arrival at the marketing office, they would be treated to their favorite drinks and snacks in a beautiful sitting area with a homelike atmosphere. Their host would sit right next to them and spend the next hour or so conversing with them about their likes and dislikes, their concerns and their questions. The host would listen for the questions that weren't asked and answer those as well. And so on . . .

I listened to Andrea talk about this idea, sitting straight up in my chair, and got more and more excited.

Why, that sounds like star treatment!

"Sure," Andrea said, "but we don't know if we can really make it happen. We're so busy around here; it might just be a pipe dream."

I went home that night and couldn't get Andrea's pipe dream out of my head.

You see, if you're like me, you haven't just had moments of wanting to feel like a celebrity . . . you've had years. While other kids were playing kick ball and jump rope, I was putting on elaborate talent shows in my backyard for the neighbors, posing for my album cover, practicing my Oscar acceptance speech, and signing autographs for anyone who asked (usually my parents).

Having turned that passion into a career as a professional speaker on the topics of employee morale and customer service, the idea of celebrity service excited me.

Of course, only celebrities really know how it feels to receive the red carpet treatment. But who, I wondered, knows how to give it?

Then it hit me! The people who serve celebrities know, of course.

So, I set about doing my research. I spent a year and a half interviewing and visiting with people who own, manage, or work for companies that cater to the Tom Cruises and the Halle Berrys of the world. The question I asked was, "What can you teach people who work in companies that don't serve the rich and famous, about giving their everyday customers celebrity-level service?"

As it turns out, plenty!

Now, I know what you're thinking. "Of course, they can give that level of service. Look at the budgets they have. Why they're serving millionaires and billionaires for goodness sake!"

True.

However, the basic principles of what they taught me are applicable whether you've got a budget for champagne or a budget for beer.

There are certain common denominators that all of the companies I researched shared. Their employees have certain tenets they live and work by, and I'm going to share them with you in this book.

Read this book and you will learn the following:

- The biggest difference between celebrities and your customers and how you can use The Chicago Pizza Principle to bridge the gap.
- How the first impressions you make on your customers can generate the same excitement as a Hollywood event in Red Carpet Arrivals.
- How getting to know your customers and Giving 'Em Their Chicken Soup will endear you to them for life.
- Ways to consistently amaze your customer, and then some, and make your customer The Star of Your Show.
- Five specific ideas for creating within your customers a sense of belonging to your business by giving them Star Power.

- How you will generate buzz and Branding Ovations when you consistently deliver the goods.
- Why, if you give genuine celebrity service, you avoid the Are You Anybody? syndrome.
- How putting your employee—or The Celebrity Next Door— first is the best path toward delivering red carpet customer service.
- When to apply The Booger Principle (you read it right) because sometimes what the customer really needs is the truth.

I will also take you where no other customer service book has taken you before. Read Be an A-List Customer to turn the tables on yourself. This chapter gives you the opportunity to consider whether or not you are a customer who rates The Celebrity Experience.

You will learn what I learned from hundreds of interviews with celebrity personal assistants, PR representatives, concierges, television executives, producers, image consultants, hair stylists, agents, red carpet escorts, craft service providers, and more. While all of these interviews add to the flavor of *The Celebrity Experience*, a few celebrity service professionals really stood out to me in terms of what they could teach us all about customer service. They are highlighted in this book.

You will meet:

Scott Graham, CEO of Xtreme Personal Assistant Concierge Services. Scott is a man with an unprecedented can-do attitude. You'll read about the amazing lengths that Scott's team will go to for their celebrity (and corporate) clients. Without the principle that Scott and his fabulous team taught me, there would be no such thing as *The Celebrity Experience*.

Jesse Itzler, co-founder of Marquis Jet. Partnered with Net-Jets, Marquis Jet provides celebrities and others with easy access to private plane travel. Jesse knows how to go the extra mile for his clients and his employees.

Rita Tateel, founder of The Celebrity Source. Rita hobnobs with the best of the best. How is she able to get so close to A-list celebrities? Because they trust her. From Rita you will learn about caring about your clients enough to tell them the truth.

Jack Canfield, author and celebrity speaker. While Jack does not work with celebrities per se, as a co-founder of the Chicken Soup for the Soul™ franchise, he is certainly a celebrity himself. He will give you some insight as to what it's truly like to receive the star treatment.

Katrina Campins and Sofia Campins of The Campins Company. Katrina is the owner of this luxury real estate company based in Miami, as well as a star of the first season of *The Apprentice*. Sophia is the sales and marketing director extraordinaire. They taught me about the power of treating your customers special, building the buzz factor, and the importance of giving back.

Gene Perret, author and comedy writer. Gene wrote comedy for Bob Hope, Carol Burnett, and other comedians of the day. His recollections of Bob Hope in particular have much to teach us about treating our employees to the red carpet treatment.

Hollywood Producer Tisha Fein; Sheri Riley, CEO of Glue, Inc.; and Jo-Ann Geffen, president of JAG Entertainment and manager to David Cassidy. Each of these people, as well as others, provided insights into the world of celebrity and how it relates to good old-fashioned customer service. I know you will enjoy, and gain much from, their anecdotes and observations.

The trick for me was to then take what I learned from the

red carpet experts and translate it into the world of everyday customer service. Luckily for me, I found a few professionals and companies out there who do not serve celebrities, but do give their customers red carpet customer service.

Meet the members of our Celebrity Experience Hall of Fame.

Tabitha Health Care Services. This not-for-profit organization, based in Nebraska, offers a continuum of care for elders from home care to assisted living and hospice. It is in our Hall of Fame for the incredible forward thinking of its leaders and staff members. Wait until you read the trolley story!

High Point University. Each time I tell someone about the incredible things going on at this university, I get a response like, "Oh, it must be a private school." Believe me, it is not the money this institution spends that makes it a Celebrity Experience provider. It is the attitude displayed regarding service to the students, the students' families, and guests.

Gaylord Opryland Resort and Convention Center Celebrity Services Department. You'll read much about the Gaylord in this book, but it was the Celebrity Services Department that truly floored me. It's not about how they treat celebrities every day, but how they treat everyday people like stars.

Dave Timmons, speaker, author, CEO of Six String Leadership, Inc. Whether in his past career as a banker or on his current path, Dave goes out of his way to make his customers and colleagues shine in his presence. You'll just love the Travis and Cody story.

Dan Maddux, executive director of The American Payroll Association. Talk about making everyday people feel like stars! Dan has made this his daily mission and, as a result, has grown his small association to a membership of 23,000. Learn what you can from this man of action!

NASCAR. There is no sports franchise that gives more

power to the fans than NASCAR racing. You can learn a lot from this organization about the power of customer engagement.

Hub Plumbing & Mechanical, Inc. Not your ordinary plumbers, these technicians literally roll out the red carpet for their customers. CEO John Wood is a man with a brand—a brand that he and his team live up to every single day.

Professional Sports Wives. Gena Pitts is nobody's sidekick. She's a life force who has built an entire business around the idea that we all deserve to have The Celebrity Experience. You'll read more about how she founded her publication and association for the wives of professional athletes.

Jobing.com. Providing localized web sites for HR recruiters and job hunters, the founders of Jobing.com decided from the start they didn't want to be just any ordinary company. They put their money where their mouths are and roll out the red carpet for their employees so they will do the same for their customers.

You will also find dozens of examples from organizations of every kind. If you work in health care, senior care, education, association management, hospitality and restaurant management, car repair, supermarkets, banking and finance, insurance, airlines, retail, coffee shops, real estate, plumbing, roofing, trades, stand-up comedy, entertainment, hotels, PR and marketing, or car rentals there are examples in this book that apply to you. If you are a leader of a Fortune 500 company, a small business, or a sole proprietor, by reading this book you will learn how to give your customers The Celebrity Experience.

Throughout the book you will find "Celebrity Sightings"—examples of professionals in a variety of occupations who have wowed their customers with red carpet customer service. You'll also get an inside look as to what it feels like to receive star treatment in the sections called "Celebrity Dish"—anecdotes by and about celebrities themselves.

Since my initial conversation with my friend Andrea, she

has moved on to another job. However, the companies and examples in this book prove that her idea was not a pipe dream. There are indeed organizations that give their customers true red carpet customer service. This book will show you how your company (and Andrea's) can become one of them.

On a Hollywood set you will find award-winning actors, fabulous scripts, flattering lighting, makeup artists, Foley (sound) artists, interesting props, and magnificent sets. However, a movie doesn't become a movie until the director gathers all of the people together, settles in his chair and yells "action!" It is only when there is action that the true Hollywood magic begins to happen. The action sections of most chapters will give you concrete steps that you can take to begin rolling out the red carpet for your customers immediately. Occasionally, you'll have to yell "cut" and "take two" . . . maybe even "take 22." That's okay. Because when it all comes together, your company will stand out as being one of only a few rare companies that truly give their customers honest-to-goodness red carpet customer service.

These days everyone is buzzing about Hollywood and its celebrities. Let's get started creating bona fide buzz for you and your business by giving everyone who walks through your doors (and on your carpet) The Celebrity Experience!

Applause!

WHEN I WAS a little girl I used to look in the mirror, hold a microphone, and practice my Academy Award acceptance speech. Okay, it was just last week and it was a hairbrush. I rehearsed everything I would say and named everyone I would thank after rushing to the stage to accept my Oscar for Best Actress.

Today it is a pen, not a microphone or even a hairbrush, that I hold in my hand. I have not won an award for best anything, but the completion of this, my first book, has been an unexpected dream come true. I finally understand why the award winners desperately want more time to thank everyone who was involved in their journey toward that incredible moment. Like any good Hollywood film, this book is, in fact, an ensemble piece, and it is with humble and honest gratitude that I thank and applaud the following stars:

God, omnipotent higher power, through which all things are possible.

My husband **Jim Cutting** for being my loving, supportive, adventurous best friend, and for giving me the time I needed to complete this book and the freedom to be myself. You are my lifetime love.

My incredible Mastermind Group, **Joan Brannick, PhD**; **Sandy Geroux**; **David Glickman**; and **Dave Timmons** for inspiring me to be a "yes" person by your examples, for cheering me on from the moment the idea for *The Celebrity Experience* hit me, for your advice and ideas, and for countless hours of reading and rereading my manuscript. In many, many ways you are the co-authors of *The Celebrity Experience*.

Rachel Street, the best assistant anyone could ever ask for, who kept the business running while I wrote this book, who cheered me on, who spent many hours helping me make deadlines, and who explored new territory in the effort to ensure this project was a huge success. You are a goddess of *The Celebrity Experience*. **Michelle Merger**, who recently joined our team and jumped right in to keep us going through the many wonderful changes in the business. You are a star performer.

Laurie Harting, my editor at Wiley, who was incredibly patient with this first-time author. With your brilliant insights you encouraged me to write a better book.

Lisa Hagan, my agent from Paraview Publishing. You are an author's dream come true, and I am looking forward to a long professional relationship and friendship.

Chellie Campbell, for introducing me to Lisa Hagan, and to **Denise O'Berry** for introducing me to Laurie Harting.

Jessica Lanagan-Peck, Shannon Vargo, Christine Kim, Linda Witzling, and everyone at Wiley. You've been wonderful to work with. The staff at **Cape Cod Compositors** for guiding me through the final edit.

Denise McCabe, who tirelessly proofread each page several times, and without whom there would be far too many commas and exclamation points in this book.

Susan RoAne, Sam Horn, Diana Booher, Greg Godek, Barbara Glanz, and Terri Kabachnick—your examples were my inspiration and the time you each spent with me helped shape the direction of my proposal and this book.

Joanne McCall of McCall Public Relations, for your energy and enthusiasm for my project. I am excited about what we can achieve together.

Oh wait, don't play the music just yet . . .

Karen Storee, Brooke Christian, and Carol Marion Smith for reading chapter after chapter and for your helpful insights. Brooke, thank you for helping to keep my name in front of prospective clients while I went into hiding.

Doug Van Dyke, Angela Bender, and David Glickman for your contributions to the title of this book.

Mom and Dad for your continuous encouragement and my sister, Juliette McCray, for helping me to edit the proposal and for your support.

Thank you to each and every person who I interviewed and visited with in researching *The Celebrity Experience*. Many of you are mentioned by name. Some of you are not. Regardless, your imprint is on this work, and I am forever grateful.

I am thankful to every Borders, Barnes and Noble, Starbucks, Panera Bread, Crispers, and coffeehouse where I spent countless hours writing and rewriting. And to Carolyn and Larry Yoss at Behind the Fence Bed & Breakfast, where I wrote the first four chapters of *The Celebrity Experience*.

Shelby Fessl, Traci Bild, Delatorro L. McNeal II, JoAnne Weiland, Scott Manthorne, Jack Canfield, Charlene Robbins, Karen Rose, and Jo-Ann Geffen for your various contributions.

Thanks also to my clients, audience members, and readers of my blog and newsletters. My energy and inspiration comes from you every day, and I am honored by the gift of working with you.

Finally, to the many theater, film, and television actors and directors who continually add joy to my life, inspire me, and make me think, feel, and laugh through their incredible work.

The Celebrity Experience

The Chicago Pizza Principle

"Yes! Yes! Yes! Yes! Yes!"
—Meg Ryan in
When Harry Met Sally

WHAT DO YOU DO when your customer asks for the seemingly impossible? Laugh? Politely decline the business? Not Scott Graham, CEO of Xtreme Personal Assistant and Concierge Services. When faced with an impossible task, Scott goes to his team and asks one question—"How?"

Want a private jet at your disposal in the next three hours? Want tickets to the Super Bowl? Need new clothes immediately because the airline lost your luggage? Xtreme Personal Assistant and Concierge Services (XPACS) is the go-to place for celebrities who are looking for someone to make the impossible possible. The following example demonstrates just how far the XPACS team will go to please its customers.

When a celebrity asked Scott to deliver a hot, fresh pepperoni pizza to his flat in London that evening, he didn't blink. The catch? The pizza was to come from a specific restaurant in Chicago, Illinois. The customer was testing him, and Scott knew it. After all, the XPACS motto is, "Anything and everything as long as it's moral, ethical and legal." Right on the web site it says, "If you can imagine it, we can deliver it." Scott and his team put their creativity to work.

If the answer was "Yes," then the question was "How?" It didn't take the XPACS team long to figure it out. They loaded up a private plane, complete with a concierge and a pizza oven. The prepared pizza was picked up in Chicago and baked as the plane was landing in London. A limo was waiting at the airport and the hot, fresh pepperoni pizza from Chicago was delivered to the customer in London, that evening and on time! If this was a test, XPACS passed. Says Scott, "The client was amazed! He told us, 'You have a client for life.' That's the kind of thing that makes you say, 'God, I *love* this job!' "

It was after hearing this story that I realized the fundamental difference between the rest of us and celebrities. For a celebrity:

Whatever the question, the answer is yes! It's the job of everyone else to figure out how.

On the other hand, the rest of us are constantly faced with a barrage of "no's."

No, you can't talk to a real person on the phone.

No, the person you're talking to can't answer that question for you and doesn't know who else can either.

No, you can't get that service here.

No, they can't tell you where to get that service.

Wouldn't you like to hear "yes" more often? I'll bet your customers would, too.

True, your customers may not have the same net worth as Scott's celebrity clients, and may not be able to afford such luxury. However, there is a lesson to be learned from high-octane service people like Scott Graham who cater to those who frequent the red carpet.

The Chicago Pizza Principle: Refrain from Saying No When the Answer Could Be *Yes!*

What if you could find a way to say yes more frequently?

What if you trained yourself and your team to think creatively when a customer has an unusual request?

What if, instead of saying no, you asked yourself how?

If you did, you'd be on your way to delivering The Celebrity Experience to your customers.

Let me tell you a story that demonstrates exactly how The Chicago Pizza Principle was applied in one of our Celebrity Experience Hall of Fame organizations. It's an incredible tale of how a team of employees at a health care organization worked tirelessly together to say yes to one of their residents when others might have just said no.

The Trolley Story

"I don't think Pat would have *let* us say no," laughs Joyce Ebmeier, the administrator for Tabitha Health Care Services, Nursing and Rehabilitation Center in Lincoln, Nebraska.

Pat, an elderly resident who lived at the skilled nursing community, had been confined to a wheelchair since she was in her 50s. Pat had taken a lot of different kinds of transportation in that wheelchair, and one day she told Joyce that she "didn't like the Tabitha bus one bit." It was an oversized van into which she had to be backed in and strapped down, and because of all the equipment, she couldn't even see out the window. Also, Pat wanted to see more people who used wheelchairs getting out into the community, but the bus took only two wheelchairs at a time. Something had to be done.

At this point, most employees of a nonprofit senior living community would have smiled and said they were sorry; it just wasn't in the budget.

Instead Joyce took the question to her staff and they started brainstorming the possibilities. Someone came up with the idea of a trolley, which Pat just loved.

The next step was to get both the president of Tabitha Health Care Services and the foundation members excited. Joyce knew that the foundation was raising money for a capital project, so most of the work would have to come from her staff.

They held a lunch for the president, the foundation members, and other VIPs of Tabitha Health Care Services. The resident, Pat, made a speech, and someone showed a PowerPoint presentation. To make a long story short, they got the green light to raise money for the trolley.

Joyce and her team, along with Pat, started with a variety of grassroots efforts. They held loose change days when the entire staff would pool its pennies and drop them in a fishbowl in the lobby. "Then the poor bus driver would have to take all that change to the bank," chuckles Joyce.

Next, a volunteer who used to be a baker for Miller & Paine Department Store stepped up to the plate. He offered to come in once a week and bake the legendary Miller & Paine cinnamon rolls. They called them "Trolley Rolls," and each week after he baked them, Pat would sit in the lobby and sell them hot and fresh to staff members and visitors, raising money for her dream.

Once they had raised about half of what was needed for the trolley, the president of Tabitha Health Care Services gave them permission to start a campaign for the rest. That's when the media got involved. Local television stations, radio shows, and newspapers began running stories about the trolley fund. A church in the community made a donation, and another church matched those funds. Soon, all of Lincoln, Nebraska, was pulling for Pat and her dream.

Finally, they had the money to purchase a used trolley they found in Florida. Second Wind Dreams, a wonderful organization that helps make dreams come true for elders living in nursing homes and assisted-living communities, kicked in the money to help bring the trolley to Nebraska.

On the day of the arrival, Pat and the rest of the residents and staff of Tabitha Health Care Services Nursing and Rehabilitation Center sat outside waiting. As the trolley pulled in, they rang bells that were given to them by Second Wind Dreams. Pat, whose health was failing by this time, was well enough to make a speech. She was the first to ring the bell and the first to ride the trolley.

Now all wheelchair-bound residents of the Tabitha community would be able to comfortably ride around the town, to the bank, and out to lunch. Because the story was in the media, residents of Lincoln, Nebraska, still smile when they see that trolley on city streets. Of course, now the entire community is always buzzing about Tabitha Health Care!

All of these great outcomes happened because some employees had the creativity and the dedication to say yes to a customer's request and then figure out how!

Saying yes is just part of the Tabitha culture. The people at Tabitha have a tradition of challenging the status quo and responding with innovation. They were:

- The first to offer Meals on Wheels in the state of Nebraska in 1967.
- The first hospice in Lincoln, Nebraska, in 1979.

- The first to offer home health care in Nebraska and the sixth in the entire country. The first in Nebraska and the second in the country to open the uniquely designed Green House Project®, a deinstitutionalized environment for skilled long-term care. Many believe this model is the future of nursing homes.

Says President and CEO Keith Fickenscher, "The thing about Tabitha is that we are never satisfied. We are always looking for the next thing. Additionally, we're teaching our 700 employees and 2,000 volunteers not to say no but instead to ask how?"

This brings us to a question. How do the innovative people who work for XPACS and Tabitha Health Care Services put The Chicago Pizza Principle to work? It starts with action!

Take One: Ask

Take Two: Choose Your Customers over Convenience

Take Three: Think Big

Take Four: Partner with Others

Take Five: Own the Problem

Take Six: Refuse to Be Satisfied

Take One: Ask

Usually the best answers come when you ask the best questions. Here are a couple of questions to ask yourself and your team as you prepare to put The Chicago Pizza Principle to work by saying yes more often and then figuring out how.

Ask what if? What if you had unlimited time, money, and resources to spend on problem solving for your customers? Now at this point, you might be thinking, "What's the point of asking that question? I don't have unlimited time, money, and resources." Maybe not. On the other hand, you don't know what's available to you until you ask. Even if the resources aren't there, by asking this question you are opening your mind up to possibilities you hadn't thought of yet. You may find yourself with answers to problems for which you thought there were no solutions.

Ask yourself, what if I could create the kind of experience for my customers that would make them feel that anything was possible? What would that look like? How would I communicate it to my customer? What if I could help my customers to feel that nothing they could ask for would be too much?

These are the questions that Maria Motsavage, president and CEO of Ideal Senior Living in Endicott, New York, asked her staff to think about when she returned from a vacation in Florida. While she was in Florida, Maria had a dining experience that changed the entire way she thinks about customer service. She was in a restaurant ordering a salad, the way she usually did—with no dressing, tomatoes, or onions and extra cheese and croutons. Typically, Maria's request would get responses like, "Sorry, the salad is already made up in the kitchen" or "There's an extra charge for the cheese." Not from this waiter! Instead, her waiter said, "When you are a guest in my house, you can have whatever you want."

Inspired by the waiter's attitude, and having enjoyed her perfect salad, Maria went back to her staff at Ideal Senior Living pumped up about giving that level of service to their residents. The question she asked, "What if we could create the feeling that our residents could have whatever they wanted in their home?" sparked a series of new actions and behaviors on the part of the employees of Ideal Senior Living that they call their Red Carpet program. You'll hear more about the program as you continue to read this book. For now, let me tell you about the results they've enjoyed as a company. In one year's time their overall satisfaction ratings in the skilled nursing center went from 26 percent to 86 percent, and over a period of four or five years employee turnover has dropped from 52 percent to 24.8 percent. This, in an industry where high employee turnover is a given.

What if you asked yourself these questions? What kind of experience could you create for your customer? What kind of results could you see in your customer and employee satisfaction scores?

Ask how? Have you ever come up with a brilliant idea just to be told, "It can't be done," "We don't do things that way here," or the dreaded, "We tried that already and it didn't work"? Have you ever found yourself thinking or uttering those words? If you have, then stop! That's right. The next time you find yourself thinking or speaking those limiting words stop yourself right then and there.

If you need to, find a physical way to remind yourself. Put a rubber band or a bracelet around your wrist. When you catch yourself saying "no" to an idea or "I can't help you" to a customer's request, take the bracelet off and put it on your other wrist. Keep doing this until you get in the habit of saying yes. Then ask yourself, "How?" How can you get this project done? What would have to happen in order for you to get the question answered? Who can solve this problem? Where can you go for answers? Brainstorm with your team. Think creatively.

As Scott Graham of XPACS told me, "I don't want my team to think out of the box. I want them to think on top of the box, under the box, around the box, on the side of the box—I want them to crush the box—do whatever they have to do to grant the customer's request." Continually move your bracelet from one wrist to the other until you find yourself in the habit of seeking answers to questions rather than assuming you don't have any.

Celebrity Dish

When the Atlanta Falcons stayed at the Gaylord Opryland Hotel they requested 15 king-size beds on one floor. They were to arrive at noon. There are usually only three king-size beds on one floor, and the housekeeping staff had to wait until guests checked out before they could change out the beds. Under the leadership of Johnny Jackson, projects coordinator, they got the "impossible" done before the football team arrived.

Take Two: Choose Your Customers over Convenience

Truth is that when someone asks us for something that is different from what we usually offer, it's human nature to shut down, explain, or make excuses for why it can't be done. We've gotten ourselves into a comfortable pattern—a rut, if you will—and it takes work and can be risky to make a change. It's just easier to do things the way we've always done them than it is to think that there might be a better way.

To give your customer The Celebrity Experience, however,

you must continually check to make sure that you are not choosing your own convenience over serving your customer in the best possible manner. Often, what is easiest for you is not going to win you any points with your customer.

While I was building my speaking practice, I also performed interactive theater shows for children around the state of Florida. One of my most frequent customers was the Public Library System. I found the youth librarians I worked with to be fun, warm, and welcoming, and I always enjoyed performing for their patrons.

Frequenting so many libraries I couldn't help but overhear the concerns that librarians had about the decreasing numbers of people who visit the library. Since bookstore chains like Borders and Barnes & Noble have popped up, more people are heading there than to the library. In fact, whenever I need a place to write, I head over to the nearest chain bookstore, buy a nonfat chai latte, and sit in the coffee shop with my laptop. Occasionally, I'll even browse the books with latte in hand.

One day, however, I decided it was time for a change, and I headed over to my local public library to write. As I walked past the gates of the lobby I encountered a sign. It read, "Absolutely NO Food or Drinks Past This Point." Okay. I expected this. I walked another 20 feet and encountered an additional sign. "Absolutely NO Food or Drinks in the Library." From the entrance to where I finally settled down to plug in my laptop, there were no fewer than five signs informing me of this policy.

Why, do you suppose, the libraries are losing business to the chain bookstores? Because when you walk into a Barnes & Noble, you can drink a cup of coffee, eat a delicious muffin, walk around the store, pull current books from the shelves, and enjoy yourself. You can even sit in a comfortable chair and read an entire book and put it back on the shelf without paying for it. The staff at Barnes & Noble allow you to do this because they know that when you are ready to purchase a book, you'll head right back to the place you are most comfortable—their store. They are creating an atmosphere and an experience for their customers.

Fortunately, many public libraries have taken the hint and are making their policies more customer friendly—even adding coffee houses to their buildings. However, this example illustrates how, while you are holding on to your convenient policies, your competitors are changing their strategies to fit the customer's desires and taking your clientele right along with them.

Remember, you certainly aren't going to wow anyone by taking the easy way out. One person who knows this well is Nido Qubein, president of High Point University. Nido has never been a person to sit back and take the easy way out. Having come to the United States as a teenager, knowing very little English and with just $50.00 to his name, he has had to work hard for everything he has earned.

Today Dr. Qubein is active on the boards of several prominent national businesses. He serves on the board of BB&T, a Fortune 500 financial corporation with $140 billion in assets and 30,000 employees; he also serves on the board of La-Z-Boy, the largest retailer of furniture in the United States, operating more than 300 furniture galleries in the United States and Canada, and recently opening galleries in Europe. In addition, he is chairman of the board of Great Harvest Bread Company, which operates 220 franchise stores in the United States. In 2005, he undertook the role of president of High Point University—his undergraduate alma mater and a liberal arts university of 3000 students in High Point, North Carolina. Nido did not get where he is today from where he came by choosing convenience.

President Qubein has made it a habit to walk around the HPU campus with his leadership team on a regular basis. While on one of these walks, he noticed a path that students had made through the grass to get to one of the buildings instead of using the beautiful brick walkways that had been provided for them. He asked his maintenance team about it, and their response was that they had tried pleading, cajoling, erecting signs, and everything they could think of to keep students from walking on the grass. Nothing had worked. "What ideas do you have?" they asked their new president.

The answer he gave surprised them. "Get a bricklayer out here and make a new path over the one the students have made." Nido realized that the students knew the path through the grass was the shortest distance from point A to point B. Of course they wanted to cut through the grass! So he took a cue from his customer. He began to look for all the other places where students had made their own paths to get where they were going, and he put brick walkways in those very spots. It wasn't easy or inexpensive, but in doing so Nido chose his customer over convenience.

Somehow it seems easier to force customers to bend to our policies and procedures than it is to create different policies that are customer friendly. In the long run, though, the customer will win out, even if it means doing business with someone else.

Which kind of service provider do you want to be?

Take Three: Think Big!

When Scott Graham put it out there to his celebrity (and corporate) customers that "If you can imagine it, we can deliver it," and that "XPACS can handle all requests from the ordinary to the extra-ordinary," he was thinking *big*. Of course, his clients think big and live large, and Scott knew that by making a promise like that he would have to do everything in his power to deliver. It's what he expects of himself and everyone who works for him.

The problem with most of us is that we're afraid to think big. We think first of all the limitations we have, and we build our customer service plans around those limitations. As I travel around the country speaking to audiences about how they can deliver Red Carpet Customer Service, I will often suggest that they buy red carpets for their businesses. One of my audience members went back to the company he worked for excited about this idea. He wanted to literally roll out the red carpet for new employees on their first day. The response he got from his coworkers was less than enthusiastic. They were concerned about mundane details like where they would store it, who would be responsible for rolling it out, and how much time would it take? My audience member's enthusiasm was deflated.

On the other hand, when I told Roger Clodfelter, Director of WOW! (yes, that's his actual title) at High Point University this story, he was aghast. "That would never happen here at HPU. Here, we think big. If we have to pull back later, we do, but we always start by thinking as big as we can. We decide what we want to do and then we create systems for getting it done." As a result, HPU is going places no college or university has gone before in terms of their customer service.

People who give The Celebrity Experience to their customers leave the small thinking to their competitors.

Celebrity Sighting

When I was speaking to a group from a hospice organization in Sacramento, California, one of my audience members told me this story. Her husband was a visiting nurse for an elderly man who was dying. This man was a huge fan of the Harry Potter franchise. He had read every book and seen every movie to date, and his home was filled with

Hogwarts memorabilia. He desperately wanted to see the newest Harry Potter movie that would be released in a few months. However, the patient was nearing the end of his life, and it was almost certain that he would not live long enough to see the movie in the theaters.

For most people, that's where the story would end. Most of us would sigh sadly as we told the tale of the patient who never got his dying wish. Not this nurse. He pulled out all the stops, called in all his connections until he finally got in touch with the producers of the movie. The nurse explained the story, pleaded with the producers, and was able to do the unthinkable. He got the producers to send him an advance copy of the movie so his patient could see it before he died. Now that's a service professional who refuses to use no as an answer.

Take Four: Partner with Others

Sometimes you aren't the one who can solve your customer's problem or fulfill a particular request, but you know that there is someone else who can. That's fine! Your job as a Celebrity Experience provider is to do whatever needs to be done to take care of your customer's needs.

How do you think Scott and the team at XPACS are able to deliver anything and everything to their customers? By partnering with others, of course. Their list of strategic partners includes every kind of business from limo services to private chefs to child care providers and sports psychologists.

Rich Santulli, CEO and founder of NetJets was able to exponentially increase his customer base when he partnered with Kenny Dichter and Jesse Itzler, co-founders of Marquis Jet. NetJets is a private aviation company that sells fractional jet ownership that works much like a time-share. Shares begin at around $400,000. Dichter and Itzler approached Santulli with their idea to sell prepaid jet cards, offering 25 hours of flight time starting at approximately $110,000. By partnering with Marquis Jet, NetJets is now able to say yes to those for whom a fractional ownership arrangement is not affordable or practical, thereby increasing its customer base.

At times you may need to partner with a competitor in order to best help your customers. Do it. If you are the one who takes the time to solve your customers' problems, even though it means sending them to someone else, nine times out of ten they'll come back to you when they need additional help.

If you don't have the answer to your customer's problem, someone else does. Find that person and you may find *you* have a customer for life.

Take Five: Own It

Is there anything more frustrating than being bounced around from one person to the next without ever getting any answers? Not likely. Just recently my husband and I had an issue with our homeowner's insurance policy. I called the insurance company and they told me to talk to the mortgage company. I called the mortgage company and they told me to call the insurance company. Arghhh! I would have been ecstatic if somebody—anybody—had taken the reins, called whoever needed to be called, and got back to me with some answers. Instead, I spent weeks trying to sort it all out, and when it was sorted out it was not to our satisfaction.

From this point forward, resolve to own whatever challenge, request, or problem is in front of you. Remove the phrases "That's not my job" and "You've got the wrong department" from your vocabulary. Stick with your customer until the problem is solved or the customer is with the person you know for sure can solve the problem. If possible, follow up. Empower your team to do whatever it takes, up to a specific dollar amount, to solve a customer's problem. Make it your personal mission to ensure all your customers have the answers they are looking for, and you'll find yourself with delighted customers.

Celebrity Sighting

Jackie Anderson shares this story of red carpet customer service she received at her local Publix Super Market:

> *It was Christmastime in 1999 in Florida, and I had several family members visiting from my hometown in Indiana for the holidays. We planned our meals, created our list, and I headed out to my local Publix Super Market.*
>
> *On my grocery list were the ingredients for a special chicken dish I created that everyone loves. I needed four packages of already cooked southwest chicken strips. I went to pick them up, but saw only two in the case. I searched everywhere in the case but couldn't find another two anywhere. I asked a nearby Publix employee if he could check in the back to see if there were any more packages stored away. He did and came back with the news that there were none.*
>
> *I explained to the clerk that I really didn't have time to travel all the way to another Publix to see if it had what I needed because I had guests waiting on me for dinner. To my amazement, he offered to drive to another nearby Publix to pick it up while I continued with my shopping!*
>
> *While I was checking out, he came back with the two packages of chicken. I thanked him profusely and was so impressed with that special red carpet service, that I let his manager know what a lifesaver he was.*
>
> *I bragged about it for weeks afterward to anyone who would listen. I still do my grocery shopping at Publix and always will.*

When you and your team get in the habit of saying yes to your customers and solving their problems creatively by asking yourself how, people will talk about you . . . and you and your company become the celebrities.

As a leader, this means gathering your team together and creating a vision of what saying yes to your customers will look like, listing the behaviors you will all need to exhibit to get there, and describing the indicators that will prove you are successful. Provide concrete examples for employees as to how they can say yes to your customers. You might want to authorize them to fix a customer problem up to a specific dollar amount. And then when your employees demonstrate the new behaviors, provide coaching if needed, but by all means reward them. Hold them up as a positive example to other employees and stimulate the spirit of competition.

When the leadership at the Gaylord Opryland Resort and Convention Center challenged its STARS (which is what employees are called at the Gaylord) to create a "Consider It Done culture," a healthy competition was sparked. Their mission? To increase guest satisfaction. Their method? To bend over backward for guests. Their gauge? To have 70 percent of customer satisfaction scores be top box (5s) by the end of 2009. (Top box is a term used to describe the highest rating on the guest satisfaction scale.)

Kevin Spivey, director of housekeeping, took the challenge very seriously. He looked at the guest satisfaction scores in his department and was not pleased. So he asked himself, "Aside from striving to do a better job of cleaning the guest rooms, how can our department positively impact guest satisfaction?" He stationed himself at a high-traffic area in the lobby, which is where, after declining bell services, people are trying to use their maps to find their rooms. Understand that the Gaylord Opryland Resort and Convention Center is a huge place, with almost 3,000 guest rooms, over 600,000 square feet of meeting space alone, and houses shops, restaurants, rivers, waterfalls, and more. Everyone who stays at the Gaylord is looking at his map at one point or another.

Kevin, who looks at every Gaylord guest as a celebrity, began to proactively ask people if they needed help finding their rooms. Then he would personally escort them, entertaining them with stories and anecdotes along the way. Soon thereafter he began to receive unsolicited letters from guests thanking him for his help. That's when it hit him. The housekeepers are probably the only other STARS, besides the valets, who know where every guest room is located.

He and Executive Housekeeping Manager Jason Davies pitched the idea to their team. Wherever they were, whatever they were doing, if any housekeepers saw guests looking at a map, or wandering around looking lost, they would stop what they were doing and approach the guests and personally guide them to where they wanted to go. And while they were doing it, they would use the time to build relationships with the guests by asking questions, sharing information about the hotel, and generally conversing with them. They would call it their "Way-Finders Program."

As their STARS said "yes" to the challenge, letters began to pour in to the Gaylord praising the housekeeping department. They put up a scoreboard and started tracking letters and rewarding the STARS that received them. It created energy, fun, and competition among the staff and the guests were happy. Within one quarter they received 100 unsolicited letters from guests.

The energy has infected the rest of the staff. For example, Suzanne Perry, director of Reservation Sales and Call Center Operations, challenged her team to find creative ways to say "yes." The result was a new enthusiasm for their Consider It Done program. When a guest calls with a special request, whether it's delivering a hot, freshly popped bowl of popcorn to a guest room, picking up prescriptions, or sprinkling rose petals on the bed, the call center employees do not delegate the task. They are on the job! They went from 0 to 128 letters in a couple of months because they were excited by the process.

And what about those overall Gaylord guest satisfaction scores? In one quarter, they went from 40 percent of their top box to an average of 59.7 percent, some weeks hitting their target goal of 70 percent. The Gaylord Entertainment Company puts its money where its mouth is. While every employee earns a $50.00 bonus each quarter if the hotel reaches its financial goals, they can earn up to $150.00 quarterly if they reach their guest satisfaction goals.

Take Six: Refuse to Be Satisfied

When you begin to work in this manner, a funny thing happens. As Keith Fickenscher of Tabitha Health Care said, "We are never satisfied." When you work in an environment of "yes," anything can happen, and you will find yourself continually trying to top yourself. This brings me to one of the perks of The Chicago Pizza Principle.

You will be challenged and you will have fun. Whether I was talking to Scott Graham of XPACS, the staffs at Tabitha Health Care and Ideal Senior Living, or the leadership team at High Point University, they all had something in common. There was an energy about them, a life force if you will, and they were falling all over themselves excitedly telling me about all they were accomplishing in their organizations. The pride they took in their work was evident.

Take on the challenge of the Chicago Pizza Principle and you might just find yourself feeling like Scott Graham of XPACS and saying, "God, I *love* this job!"

Celebrity Sighting

In order to manufacture lenses to the correct power or RX, Pearle Vision employees use a piece of machinery called a polisher or cylinder machine. When Rick, a Pearle Vision employee, called Practical Systems, Inc. (PSI), to tell them the pump on his polisher wasn't working, he was understandably upset because his company promises customers they will receive their eyeglasses in one hour. Without a working pump, Rick could not honor this promise. Thanks to an employee who practices The Chicago Pizza Principle, Rick did not have to worry. Here's the letter Rick wrote to Practical Systems.

> Our pump went down and we were out of business. Missy Hoffman, our PSI sales rep, saved the day. She could have told us she would send the pump overnight, but instead, got in her car and drove over 100 miles to get us the pump that day. We were "wowed" by her customer service. It says a lot about Missy and PSI that they would do that for a customer.
>
> In this business there are a lot of people selling products, but it is outstanding service that keeps us going. That is how we stay in business against the large retailer in our shopping plaza and that is why we give our business to PSI.
>
> Rick
> Pearle Vision, Sanford, Florida

A word about boundaries: Whenever I speak on the topic of The Chicago Pizza Principle someone always approaches me and says, "We can't give our customers *everything* they want." It is true that in some situations you have to tell your customer, "No." Even celebrities tire of being yes'd to death, and respond well to people who respect them enough to kindly tell them the truth. See the chapter entitled "The Booger Principle" for a more detailed explanation.

You will probably run across a few customers who take advantage of your reputation for saying yes. Some customers are so demanding that pleasing them isn't worth the time or trouble. By all means, in those select cases, set your boundaries.

But I'll bet you find most customers are surprised and delighted when you go out of your way just a little bit. And you, in turn, will be delighted to help them.

Remember, if you truly want to give red carpet customer service and treat your customers as if they were stars, the general rule of thumb should be whatever the question, the answer is "Yes!" It's then up to you to figure out how.

Before I close this chapter, let's go back to the Tabitha Health Care Services and Pat's dream for a trolley. Here's how the story ended.

Two months after the trolley was delivered, Pat passed away. The trolley was taken to the funeral service, and her family rode it from the church to her gravesite. Her great-granddaughter rang the bell the entire way. Everyone in the city of Lincoln, Nebraska, knew that trolley was one of Pat's great accomplishments.

"And we were better as a community because of it," says Joyce. "We became better people because Pat had a great dream to which our employees and volunteers said, 'Yes,' and then figured out how!"

And you will become a better service professional or a better company by learning from The Chicago Pizza Principle and making it a habit to say, "Yes!"

Red Carpet Arrivals

EVERY FEBRUARY I SETTLE in to watch the Academy Awards. My favorite part? The red carpet arrivals, of course.

The people at the Kodak Theatre, where the ceremony has been held since 2002, spend weeks in preparation, rolling out the carpet, putting up the velvet ropes, and hanging drapes to cover the storefronts that usually line the grand staircase. It's all about making the nominees feel special on the night many of them have been dreaming about all of their lives. From the moment their limos pull up to the curb, everything focuses on the stars. They step out onto the carpet and are greeted by the official Academy Red Carpet Celebrity Greeter (in 2007 it was Robert Osborne, film historian and *Hollywood Reporter* columnist), who has spent the entire year getting to know everything about everyone he will be welcoming that evening. He announces their names, and there are 600 fans in bleacher seats who collectively roar in appreciation. As the celebrities walk the carpet, there are photographers lined up to take their photos and interviewers raving over their accomplishments and asking, "Who are you wearing?" and exclaiming, "You look ravishing!"

There is an atmosphere of excitement and a reverence for the ceremony seen almost nowhere else.

I can't imagine it would feel as special if the nominees simply parked in a lot, opened the door to the theater, stepped inside, and took their seats. No, this occasion is far too significant for such an ordinary arrival.

What about the welcome you give your patrons? Are they getting the impression that you are excited to see them or that they are just anonymous customers coming through your door?

Imagine the bona fide buzz you'd create about your business if you welcomed your customers through your doors as if they were Hollywood celebrities nominated for Academy Awards. Garrett Richter, president and CEO of First National Bank of Florida, put it best when he said, "If we roll out the red carpet for billionaires, they won't even notice. If we roll it out for millionaires, they expect it. If we roll out the red carpet for thousandaires, they appreciate it. And if we roll out the red carpet for hundredaires, they tell everybody they know."

Let me tell you how two of our Celebrity Experience Hall of Fame members roll out the red carpet for their guests.

University of WOW!

No member of the National Speakers Association, or regular attendee of its national conference can help but know the name of Nido Qubein. He is well loved in our organization, having launched the NSA Foundation that gives financial assistance to members who find themselves in need. He is loved for his charm, his snappy, well-tailored suits, his kindness, and his knowledge. Nido is talked about within the National Speakers Association. So, it didn't take long for the buzz about all the incredible things he was doing as the new president of High Point University in North Carolina to reach my ears. Wanting to know more, I asked Nido for a tour of the campus, and he graciously agreed.

I was put in touch with Andy Bills, vice president for student enrollment and Christopher Dudley, vice president for community relations, who responded to my request for an appointment immediately. As a matter of fact, each time I sent an e-mail or made a phone call with a question or a confirmation, it was responded to immediately and with enthusiasm. As I checked into my hotel room in High Point, North Carolina, the night before my tour, I logged onto my e-mail to find a message from Mr. Bills telling me how much they were looking forward to my visit.

The next morning, as I drove on to the campus, I came to a circular drive with an absolutely gorgeous fountain in the middle. There, in the grass, designating my parking space, was a beautiful sign proclaiming, "High Point University Welcomes Special Guest Donna Cutting." Was this just for me, because I'm an author writing a book about celebrity service? No. I saw that *all* visitors coming that day had their own signs and their own parking spaces. I was so impressed, I took a picture of mine. Later, Mr. Bills told me that almost everyone poses for a photo by their sign.

Since I was early, I decided to walk around before going into the Wrenn Building where I was to meet Mr. Bills. It wasn't 30 seconds before I noticed a sharply dressed man coming my way. It was my host. He was expecting me. We entered the building, and there was my name again, on a flat screen television above the welcome desk, along with the names of others who would be visiting that day. Laney Morris, campus visit coordinator, was waiting to give me a warm welcome, greeting me by name . . . of course. To one side was a beautifully decorated parlor with a fireplace, comfortable couches and chairs, and refreshments. The parlor is where prospective students and their families wait for their tours, and Laney's sole job is to make them feel welcomed and appreciated. She is also the *real* person who answers the phone when you call. No automated phone systems at HPU.

Prospective students and their family members are taken on tours that include no more than a couple of families at a time, in order to give them each the special attention they deserve. Student guides are given information about the interests of each prospective student, so they can tailor the tour accordingly. My tour guide, Andy, knew that I had a degree in theater arts so he took me to see the beautiful Hayworth Fine Arts Center where students were preparing for opening night. Ahhh, home! We skipped the science building. Did I mention all visitors are driven around in a golf cart? Okay, it's not a limo, but when you've spent the last week walking the expansive campuses of other universities, it is a welcomed change.

Before they leave, visitors are given a big, beautifully designed box of HPU goodies to take home. Mine included a T-shirt, a baseball cap, snacks, a Starbucks gift certificate, and information about the university. You can't help but walk away feeling as though you've been treated like the most important person in the world.

Is their High Point hospitality working? You decide. Since they started their efforts, campus visits went up 70 percent, and in 2006, enrollment was up 63 percent in three years time. And it gets better. In 2007, campus visits from high school juniors doubled, and as of this writing they have 250 more deposits for the freshman class of 2007 than they had in 2006. There is no doubt their red carpet service is creating a buzz and having a positive effect on the bottom line.

Flawless Service with Celebrity Flair

Pam Huff, director of Celebrity Services for the Gaylord Opryland Resort and Convention Center in Nashville, Tennessee, is the go-to person for famous musicians, Hollywood movie stars, and sports personalities who stay at the hotel. Whether the Pointer Sisters need balsamic vinegar for their salads, David Cassidy needs someone to shield him in the elevator from overzealous 40-year-old female fans, or Bill Cosby needs someone to answer his telephone, Pam and her team of nine Celebrity Services STARS are on the job!

However, it's their celebrity treatment of those of us who *aren't* famous that has earned them a spot in our Celebrity Experience Hall of Fame.

When, in 2001, the leadership team at Gaylord Entertainment Company wanted to break the paradigm of what constitutes exceptional service, their talk turned to the corporations and organizations that hold their conventions at their hotels. (Gaylord currently has resort properties in Nashville, Florida, and Texas and will soon open another in Maryland). Eighty percent of the business at the Opryland resort is conventions and meetings while 20 percent comes from individual families and guests there for leisure. The leadership team started throwing around ideas about what would truly wow meeting planners who were visiting their hotel as a potential convention site. It was during this discussion that the idea of the Celebrity Services Department was born.

If you were a meeting professional holding your convention at the Gaylord Opryland Resort and Convention Center, you would be put in touch with Pam Huff and Celebrity Services. You'd be asked to name the VIPs and celebrities within your group. You might name the CEO of your company, your board of directors, your special speakers, or volunteers who have been integral in planning the meeting. Whoever you named would be given the red carpet treatment.

When I interviewed Pam by telephone about Celebrity Services at Gaylord Opryland, I was impressed. From the actual red carpet, to the limos, to the amenities, it all sounded amazing.

Then Pam invited me to stay at Gaylord Opryland, and I was given a real understanding of the unique experience they provide for those convention VIPs and celebrities. The Gaylord Celebrity Services Department has the idea of red carpet arrivals down cold. As you read about my experience, use it to spark your own creative juices about what you could be doing to truly wow your customers upon their arrival at your business.

Prior to my arrival, I was called by Christa Harris, one of the Celebrity Services STARS (as the Gaylord Entertainment Company refers to their employees). She wanted to know my snack preferences, all about my hobbies, and whether I preferred a massage or a facial. Ah, decisions, decisions! Upon my arrival at the airport, Celebrity Services STAR Scott Johnson was waiting for me. He helped me retrieve my luggage and showed me to the black stretch limo that would take us to the hotel. When we got to the hotel, what a reception awaited us! A valet waved the limo into a particular spot, and five or six uniformed Celebrity Services STARS and valets were gathered to meet and greet me. The limo door was opened, and a flashbulb went off. I had my own paparazzi! (The photographer is offered as an option for celebrity service guests, but not an automatic feature. Pam knew that I would want to document the experience.)

I was helped onto the long red carpet and was introduced around, each person welcoming me as "Ms. Cutting." Scott checked me in, and he and Christa immediately took me up to my suite. The Gaylord Opryland has several suites that are available for meeting professionals and those they designate as celebrity guests.

Everything I had mentioned to Christa on the telephone in terms of my preferences was available for my use, and then some. They had my favorite drinks and snacks, the green tea I had asked for, and even my favorite magazines. I'll go into detail on this in the chapter called "Give 'Em Their Chicken Soup," but for now let me tell you what really floored me. At the time, I was on a special diet that had me making smoothies twice a day using spring water, ice, and some other ingredients. I had not asked them to provide a special kind of ice, but they thought of it themselves. Prior to my arrival, they had bought bags of ice made of purified spring water at a local health food store. Each morning, at the time I specified, the dietary department brought fresh ice, reserved just for me, to my door.

Throughout my stay, the Celebrity Services team continued to amaze me. Once I had settled into my room, I noticed the message light blinking on my phone. It was from Daniel Di Giacomo, another one of the STARS, who informed me he would be my personal concierge during my stay. I asked him for a wakeup call, and the next morning I received my call promptly at 6:00 A.M. At 6:01 A.M., I received a call from Daniel—checking to make sure I'd received the first one!

The next day my schedule was jam-packed with meetings and interviews with a variety of Gaylord STARS. And the surprises continued. My favorite surprise occurred when I was going from the Celebrity Services office back to the Old Hickory Library where I was conducting my interviews. As we rounded the corner, I noticed about 75 employees (or STARS) standing on the staircase and lining the hallway. I assumed they were posing for a group photograph, but then they began to applaud and I realized they were there for me. They were giving me what they call a STAR Ovation. When a special guest (such as a meeting planner who's holding a convention at the hotel) is on-site, any hotel STAR can e-mail the rest of the STARS and spread the word to meet at the grand staircase or any other location at a certain time. When these special guests arrive, they are greeted with STAR Ovations. My favorite part of the ovation was seeing how excited the STARS were when they saw how moved I was. Could you use a similar idea to delight your customers and excite your employees?

After having my own star turn at the Gaylord, I wanted to know what the resort's actual customers and prospective customers experienced. So I called Caroline Proctor, whose company had just bought out the entire hotel for its May 2008 worldwide conference.

I asked Caroline how her experience at the Gaylord stacked up to those at other hotels. "Over the top," she said. "In fact, traveling with me on this site visit was the director of events for this company. She's been booking hotels for conventions for over 15 years, and she was completely blown away. She told me that in her entire career this was by far the best experience she'd ever had."

Aside from the limo pickup and the red carpet arrival, Caroline and her team were treated to tickets to Opryland and backstage passes. "We also got tickets to see *Nashville Star* (the country version of *American Idol*). We walked through the stage door to get in and walked across the stage to get to our seats. We met the celebrities afterward. And it was all a total surprise from the Celebrity Services Department."

One day, according to Caroline, "they provided lunch for us in a private room at the Wildhorse Saloon, one of Gaylord's downtown restaurants. In the middle of lunch, platinum-selling band Blackhawk came in and sang acoustic just for the five of us. And another time, when we were having breakfast on a balcony overlooking the river on the Gaylord property, a boat stopped by our table and a rock singer with a guitar serenaded us."

As a result of her experience with the Celebrity Services Department at the Gaylord Opryland Resort and Convention Center, Caroline's company not only booked that hotel, but plans in the future to hold another convention at the Gaylord National, a property currently under construction in Maryland.

The executive director of national accounts for Gaylord drove an hour to Caroline's office to take her to the Gaylord National construction site. When they pulled up to a trailer, Caroline was greeted outside by Gaylord STARS. Inside the trailer was a beautiful table set with white linen tablecloths, gourmet food, and waiters. "I couldn't believe they were pulling this off on a construction site," Caroline told me. "I even received a personalized hard hat. They are a total class act."

Pam Huff and her Celebrity Services STARS just keep getting better. In 2002, after the service was developed, 13 percent of postconvention survey respondents specifically named Pam's department as integral to the success of their conference. By 2006, that number grew to 75 percent, and as of this writing in 2007, they have already surpassed their record. And with conventions accounting for the majority of its business, the Gaylord Opryland Resort and Convention Center is at 80 percent or greater occupancy at all times. According to General Manager Arthur Keith, this is almost unheard of in the hotel industry.

And what the Gaylord Opryland Celebrity Services Department and High Point University leaders know is this: It's the first impressions that you make on a customer that lay the foundation for the rest of the relationship.

How can you make a smashing first impression with red carpet arrivals? It takes action!

Take One: Pull Out All the Stops

Take Two: Put their Name on the Marquee

Take Three: It Starts *Before* the Curtain Goes Up

Take Four: Be Unique and Unforgettable

Take Five: Never Let It End

Take One: Pull Out All the Stops

Gather your team and ask yourselves this question: What would it be like if we pulled out all the stops the next time a new customer called on our place of business? How could we create such an impression, the first time around, that they would come back again and again, bringing everyone they knew with them? Here are some of the lessons that can be learned from High Point University, the Gaylord Opryland Hotel Celebrity Services Department, and, yes, the Academy Awards.

Be there to greet them. We've all been there, haven't we? Walking through the aisles of a department store with a question and not finding someone to help us. Calling a company or business hoping to speak to a live person, only to be met with an automated telephone service. Frustrating, isn't it? You might think to yourself, "Don't they want my business?"

Organizations like High Point University have bucked this trend by hiring someone specifically to welcome visitors and make them feel wanted and comfortable. The red carpet at the Academy Awards would not have that same air of excitement if there weren't an official greeter to announce the celebrities' names that prompt the roar of the crowd.

Katrina Campins, star of the first season of *The Apprentice* and founder of the Campins Company, a luxury real estate business based in Miami, has this to say: "I think companies can learn to create that welcoming feel by having someone to specifically cultivate customer relationships." She has done so by hiring her mother, Sofia, as sales and marketing director and she is the first person you reach when you contact Katrina's office. From my own experience I can tell you it works! While setting up the interview I had with Katrina, communications went mainly through Sofia, once by phone and mostly via e-mail. I will tell you, I have never experienced someone who could make me feel all warm and fuzzy by what she writes in an e-mail quite like Sofia can. I have never met her, and yet she made me feel as though she were my friend and my fan from our first communication.

Ken Blanchard has written a fantastic book called *Raving Fans*. In the book, Blanchard uses a parable to demonstrate that if you want to build buzz about your business, you've got to give your customers something to buzz about—extraordinary service. Through her exemplary service, Sofia showed me that if you want to make raving fans of your customers, you need to first demonstrate that you are your customers' raving fan.

Even if you are not in charge of hiring an official greeter, you can do your part. Make it your mission to be awake, alert, and ready with a warm smile and a friendly hello for everyone you encounter in your workday. Be present, available, and ready to help them if they need it. (That said, beware of being too intrusive. There are clothing stores I will no longer frequent because the salesperson stalked me like a paparazzi, commenting on every item I looked at.) For instance, when the staff members at Ideal Senior Living come within 10 feet of anyone, they make eye contact, and within 5 feet, it's a pleasant verbal exchange. Using these guidelines makes it routine at their community to acknowledge anyone who walks in their door.

Even if you have an official greeter on your team, what's most effective is when everyone is there and ready to welcome your customers. Imagine if you were a celebrity guest at the Gaylord Opryland Hotel, and you were driven up to the lobby entrance to find a whole team of people there awaiting your arrival. When the freshman class arrives for their first day at High Point University, parents stay in the car. Students and faculty line up to unload their cars and help the newcomers move into their dorm rooms. That kind of pomp and circumstance generates an air of excitement that customers will go back and talk about.

Let's say you don't have the kind of business where people come to your venue, but rather the first impression they receive is on the telephone. You can stand out from your competition immensely by having a real person answer your phone. John Wood, CEO of Hub Plumbing & Mechanical, a member of our Celebrity Experience Hall of Fame, promises his customers that he is available for them 24 hours a day, 7 days a week. To that end he has hired someone specifically to answer the phones during the day, as well as in the evenings and on the weekend. Having a real person there for his customers has often made the difference between John getting the business instead of his competition. In this day and age, having a real person on the line instead of a machine can really make your business stand out.

Give them swag. When I asked people who serve celebrities for their definition of star treatment, many people replied with one word: swag. It isn't unusual for celebrities to be given expensive gifts by their fans and others. It's ironic that some of the wealthiest people in the world rarely get asked to pay for anything. Katrina Campins told me about some of her experiences resulting from her celebrity as a cast member of *The Apprentice*. "We [the cast] would all go to dinner and it would be paid for, or we'd walk into a store and they would tell us, 'Whatever you want, it's taken care of.' I thought to myself, 'If this is how they're treating me, imagine what Angelina Jolie is getting.'"

Even at the awards ceremonies, nominees walk away with gift baskets filled with swag, expensive gifts, trips, spa certificates, and the latest and greatest gadgets on the market.

However, there is a solid business reason why celebrities are given so many goodies. It's because when they wear or use or talk about a product or service, it creates a buzz that money can't buy. Once a celebrity is seen using a product, sales go up exponentially. When Katrina wore a watch on *The Apprentice* that was given to her by Jacob the Jeweler, she could hardly believe how many men called her asking where they could buy one for their wives.

While I realize that your customers may not be as much in the limelight as other celebrities, you can still create buzz by incorporating a little swag into your welcome. A box of goodies, a welcome basket, a free T-shirt, a gift card—all of these things go a long way toward making your customers feel as though they've been treated like someone special. And when you've made them feel special, they will tell all their friends. Why, even now, as I sit here at Starbucks and write, I'm wearing my HPU T-shirt. Even though new and prospective students are gifted with all this swag, the campus bookstore reported a 70 percent increase in sales of HPU merchandise in 2006 from 2005.

In 2004, the Promotional Products Association International published a study entitled "Promotional Products: Impact, Exposure and Influence, A Survey of Business Travelers at DFW Airport." Here are its findings:

- 55 percent of people questioned said they keep their promotional products for more than one year.
- 76.1 percent of respondents could recall the advertiser's name on the promotional product that they had received within the past 12 months.
- 75.4 percent of respondents said they kept their promotional products because they were useful.

Promotional Products Association International, 2004

Take a look at the lines outside the door of your local Ben & Jerry's ice cream shop next April when they hold their annual Free Cone Day. Check out the mentions they receive in the media on that day to see how much buzz you could create for *your* business by giving a few items away. It's just that kind of buzz that enabled a small scoop shop housed in a renovated gas station to grow to a $4 million business in six short years. And in 2000, Ben & Jerry's was sold to Unilever for $326 million.

While you're thinking about the swag you can incorporate into your customer's welcome, think about the trimmings that signify that something is a real event. While trimmings and decorations don't make for exceptional customer service, they certainly do add a sense of occasion to the event. Literally roll out a red carpet, put up some velvet ropes, and make people feel as if they are stars. Send your best car to pick someone up. Treat all customers as though they deserve the best, because if you do they will come back . . . with more customers.

Take Two: Put Their Name on the Marquee

As I've mentioned before, when I was performing interactive theater shows for children, I presented at a lot of public libraries. The youth librarians were all wonderful to work with; however, there are a few that stand out in my mind because of the way they used their creativity to make me feel special. One, in particular, would reserve a parking space for me with a sign using the name of whatever character I was portraying that day. One year it was "Reserved for Filomena the Fairy Godmother," and the next time it read, "Reserved for Pirate Jenny." I was tickled pink to receive such star treatment. I was reminded of this when I saw my name on the sign at High Point University holding my parking space, and then again on the flat screen TV in the welcome center. Nothing sounds as sweet as hearing your name pass through someone's lips or seeing your name in print.

Let your customers know that you know them:

Reserve parking spaces for people using their names.

Put banners up welcoming guests by name.

Put the names of your customers on the outside marquee.

Put the names of your customers on your menu, web site, and company literature.

Picture this: You bring a group of friends to McCormick & Schmick's Seafood Restaurant in the Mall at Millenia in Orlando, Florida, to celebrate your birthday. You might just find that they have printed up special birthday menus with *your* name all over them.

One of the surprises that impressed celebrity guest Caroline Proctor so much about her visit to the Gaylord Opryland Hotel is that when she checked into her room, all the televisions were set to a screen that showed her company logo. "Even better," says Caroline, "the desserts we were served at the hotel's Old Hickory Steakhouse were branded with our company logo. Can you believe it? The pastry chef goes as far as branding the dessert with our logo!"

Just greeting someone by name makes quite a difference in personalizing the service you give them and keeps you both engaged in the conversation. This is such an important ingredient to the Celebrity Experience that we will be addressing it in other chapters as well. For now, ask yourself, "In what creative ways can we use the names of people to really wow those who are learning about our company for the first time?"

Take Three: It Starts Before the Curtain Goes Up

First impressions often start long before your customers ever meet you in person. What are you doing *before* you meet them to make your prospective clients feel comfortable and safe and excited about working with you? If you were to call Hub Plumbing & Mechanical to schedule some work, you would receive an e-mail from your plumber a few days prior to his visit. It would include his picture, the approximate time of his arrival and a little bit about him, his family, hobbies, and so forth. As a result, customers are much more comfortable opening the door to the plumber. He's not a stranger, because they've been "introduced" to him before.

The several e-mails I received from Mr. Bills and Mr. Dudley from High Point University, telling me how excited they were about my upcoming visit, made a great impression on me before I ever pulled into the driveway.

When His Eminence Archbishop Demetrios and other dignitaries from the Greek Orthodox Church were to visit the Gaylord Opryland Resort, Celebrity Service STAR Billie Stoops spent hours prior to their visit on research. She and the rest of the STARS who would come in contact with the group had to know everything about them beginning with how to address them, the customary greetings, and their dietary requirements, right down to the significance of each ceremonial robe and cane. She trained others in the hotel, repeatedly going over each name so all staff members would pronounce them correctly. The result was their trademark flawless service. Billie, who was visibly moved by the experience, remarked, "The work we did for those guests reminded me of my purpose. I had a clearer understanding of why I do what I do."

Think about how you are setting the stage for your first interaction with your customers, getting them as excited about meeting you as you are about meeting them.

Take Four: Be Unique and Unforgettable

Work to welcome your customers in a way that your competitors won't. When prospective students visit High Point University, they are taken to the president's office as part of the tour. When they get there, they are warmly greeted by Judy Ray, administrative assistant to the president. In front of her desk they will discover a gum ball machine, and on her desk is a bowl full of quarters. Visitors are encouraged to take a quarter and get a gumball, which creates laughter and all manner of conversation about favorite colors and flavors. If President Nido Qubein hears this going on, he will come out of his office and personally greet his guests. He then bets them that they won't meet another university president at any of the other campuses they visit. If they do, he says, they should write him and he'll send them one dollar. If they don't, he jokes that he wants them to send him a dollar. While I was visiting, Judy showed me several letters that came from visitors thanking them for the tour. Included with the letters? One dollar bills, of course!

Here's a brainstorm question for you: What could you—only you—do when you greet a new or prospective customer that would be different from what everyone else is doing? If you work in a restaurant, what could you do differently? If you are a realtor, what unique way could you greet prospective clients?

Whatever your business, try to come up with that one unique experience that will have your prospective customers saying, "Of all the places we visited, they were the only ones who (you fill in the blank)." It is your uniqueness that makes you and your company unforgettable.

For instance:

- The Gaylord Opryland Resort and Hotel is the only hotel where you can get a wake-up message from Vince Gill, Pam

Tillis, or Trace Adkins through their new service called, "Waking with the Stars."

- Hub Plumbing & Mechanical is the only plumbing company that sends out its plumbers in red trucks, in red uniforms, with red carpets to lay out their tools on, 24 hours a day, 365 days a year.
- The Lost Sock is the only laundromat in Richmond, Virginia, that has open mike night once a week. They have a bar and a deli as well, and patrons are invited to bring their guitars and a basket of dirty clothes.
- National Amusements, operators of over 1,500 cinema houses, offers the only movie theaters where you can get reserved seating, rocking recliners, ushers who show you to your seat and live music while you wait for the movie to begin.
- Enterprise built its brand on being the only rental car company that will pick you up wherever you are and drive you to its lot.

Take Five: Never Let It End

Of course, once you've rolled out the red carpet for your customers, it's important that you don't let it end there. At High Point University they are diligent about what they call the "wraparound" for each experience they give their visitors and students. In my case, I received a lovely handwritten note from Andy Bills, thanking me for my visit. Included with the note was a gift card for Great Harvest Bread Company, of which Nido Qubein is chairman. Other visitors receive a note and gift card, as well as a personalized letter from the chair of the department that interested them. When they invite scholarship recipients to tour the university, President Qubein talks to them about the difference between Hershey Kisses and Godiva chocolates, calling his guests "Godivas." When they return home there is a beautifully wrapped box of—you guessed it—Godiva chocolates, waiting for them. With it is a note that states, "You are a Godiva."

Celebrity Dish

Steve Gerardi of Sunshine Promotions loves to book Melissa Etheridge, Bonnie Raitt, and Reba McEntire. After a concert, they always send *him* cookies or flowers to thank him for the booking.

When a celebrity guest leaves the Gaylord Opryland Hotel, Pam Huff schedules one of her STARS to be there, even if it's 5 o'clock in the morning. "They escort the guest to the lobby, assist them with luggage, and wish them a safe journey home. There will be a thank-you note sent to their home or business shortly. Also, once they have visited our hotel, we have their profile in our system. That information is shared with all Gaylord Celebrity Service Departments, so whether that person is in Texas or Florida or Nashville they will always be treated to the red carpet service."

Of course, once you have introduced customers to your business, you will want them to continue feeling that they are being treated like royalty every time they return. We'll address that in future chapters.

Celebrity Sighting

Every year, the National Speakers Association (NSA) has an annual convention, usually in July and in rotating locations. Within the last five years, it's been held in Orlando, Florida, twice, which makes the Central Florida chapter the host for the convention. The host chapter will usually have a hospitality booth, complete with music, snacks, and trinkets to give away having to do with the local area. When the convention was to be held in Orlando in 2002, Ed Peters was the president of the Central Florida chapter, and he decided that he wanted to give the attendees a welcome unlike any they had ever seen.

It started before they ever arrived. The chapter members posed for a photo wearing tropical shirts and holding a banner that read "Orange You Glad You're Coming to Florida?" The photo was made into 4,000 postcards, which NSA-CF chapter members divided up to personalize with handwritten notes and send to every member of the national organization.

On the day those NSA board members and other VIPs of the organization began to arrive, Central Florida chapter members cleaned up their cars and headed to the airport. There, the volunteers met all the VIPs at their gates, helped them retrieve their luggage, and drove them to the hotel. Up until that point no other chapter had gone quite so far with their welcome. To ensure that all attendees got a tropically customized version of the red carpet treatment, Ed went so far as to have a truckload of sand brought into the hotel lobby to create a beach and asked talented chapter member, Nancy Street, to build a tiki hut. On the first day of the convention, attendees were warmly welcomed on the "beach" by Central Florida chapter members who gave them a big smile and a bottle of suntan lotion (a huge hit), all to the beat of steel drums—sponsored by the chapter.

On the final day of the convention, attendees walking out of the last general session were treated to a standing ovation by members of the host chapter, who were standing on chairs, applauding, hooting, and hollering. The leaders of the organization continue to rave about the welcome they receive whenever they come to Central Florida.

3

Give 'Em Their Chicken Soup

WHEN MARIAH CAREY PERFORMS, several 16-ounce plastic bottles of Evian are the only acceptable water for her dressing room.

When Vice President Dick Cheney arrives at his hotel suite, the decaffeinated coffee is brewing, four Diet Sprites are chilling, and all televisions are tuned to the Fox network.

Eminem requests a Ping-Pong table, and Marilyn Manson a personal butler.

Whether it's their favorite hard-to-find beverage, the furniture draped in white sheets (as one starlet requests), or a continually topped off jar of blue candy, all celebrities have their favorite items or conditions that make them feel comfortable and special.

Even when it's not in their contract, celebrities are used to being showered with gifts and goodies that are personal and meaningful to them.

Jack Canfield is the author of *The Success Principles™*, *The Aladdin Factor*, and *You've Got To Read This Book!* He's probably best known for the *Chicken Soup for the Soul™* series, which he co-founded with Mark Victor Hansen.

43

An extremely down-to-earth man, Jack practices what he preaches and does not have a long rider listing all of the items he must have in his hotel room when he speaks. However, he is a celebrity who is well-loved, and, as a result, people go out of their way to make him feel special.

While I was researching this book, I had an opportunity to talk with Jack about the extra lengths that people will go to surprise and delight him. Here, Jack describes one particular example that really touched him.

I've often had the opportunity to stay at the Ritz-Carlton.

The motto of the Ritz-Carlton is, "We are ladies and gentlemen serving ladies and gentlemen."

I stayed at a Ritz-Carlton in Chicago when I was on my book tour. When I checked in, I got to my room and there was a thermos bottle on a table with a little card that said, "Chicken Soup for Jack Canfield's Body and Soul." They had made chicken soup and put it in a thermos so it was hot when I got there. Alongside it there was a bowl and a spoon and a napkin, all very nicely laid out.

It was just that little extra touch that made me feel special. You know, the chicken soup may have been something that was already on their menu, and I don't know how much effort they really went to . . . but what was special was the fact that they made something that personalized the experience just for me. They knew who I was, and they reached out.

Why not give your customers their Chicken Soup? It's that little personal touch that pertains only to them alone and shows that you are paying attention. And it makes you *unforgettable*.

What is their Chicken Soup? It's different for each customer. It's the tangible (or intangible) ways that you let your customers know that you know them personally and that you're looking out for them. It's a way you can be unforgettable, in a good way, in the eyes of your customer.

Know this: The more specific the service, the more terrific the service.

Giving your customers their Chicken Soup is a way of getting specific with your service.

Celebrity Dish

When Jesse Itzler, co-founder of Marquis Jet, learned that Matt Damon was flying home after wrapping up his latest film he sent along a bottle of Matt's favorite wine with a congratulatory note for the flight. Says Jesse, "It's about the little things you do that the customer doesn't expect."

"Wait," you're saying, "That would be a great idea if I worked in a hotel chain. It won't work for my business."

Wrong! In the "Celebrity Sightings" section of this chapter, you'll find several examples of how this principle has been applied in a variety of work situations. However, let me share with you one of my favorite stories that comes from a person who is better than anyone I know at giving people their chicken soup.

These Are for Travis and Cody

His name is Dave Timmons, and he is an author, speaker, musician, and the CEO of Six String Leadership, Inc., one of the companies in our Celebrity Experience Hall of Fame. In years past, however, he was a successful banker.

At the time of this story, Dave had just been promoted to manager of the largest commercial banking center of a major bank in Indianapolis, Indiana.

As a new manager, Dave was eager to make his bank successful by bringing in significant new business. To that end, one of his goals was to land Mr. C. as a customer for the bank. Mr. C. was a very prominent businessman in Indianapolis and had been on the bank's prospect list for years. However, none of the previous managers had been able to get business from him.

Undaunted by the record of his predecessors, Dave made an appointment to call on Mr. C. to once again offer some of the bank's services.

As Dave tells it, "When his secretary brought me into his office for the first time, I heard his voice, but I did not see him. Mr. C. was sitting behind a hand-carved desk in the shape of an eagle, elevated on a tall platform. The room was rather dark and the only thing I could see behind the desk was the red end of a lit cigarette."

When Mr. C. spoke, he asked, "Are you Dave Timmons, the man from the bank?"

Dave answered, "Yes."

"You will have five minutes of my time. I will ask all of the questions. If I like your answers, you may have a chance to come back and see me."

He then directed Dave to sit in the middle of three chairs against the wall. The middle chair had a spotlight directed at it. Mr. C. used the five minutes to interrogate Dave with a series of rapid-fire questions and soon the time was up.

That was Dave's first call.

Apparently he answered the questions to Mr. C.'s liking, because in a month Dave had the chance to call on him again.

This time he got 15 minutes and was allowed to ask some questions. "I still wasn't even close to earning his business. I was just warming him up."

"On my third call," says Dave, "I decided to stop talking about banking, loans, and deposits and find out more about him as a person. In the course of the conversation Mr. C. made an offhand remark that he had to leave early because he was taking his grandsons, Travis and Cody, to the Indianapolis Indians baseball game that evening. More than anything else he loved taking his grandsons to the Indians game."

Well, it just so happened that the Triple-A Indianapolis Indians were customers of Dave's bank. It was also true that Dave sat on one of the team's local boards.

Dave began to put his connections to work.

When he went back to visit Mr. C. the fourth time, their once icy relationship was slowly warming up as evidenced by two facts: 1. Mr. C. had moved to one of the three chairs next to Dave. 2. The spotlight was replaced by normal room lighting.

So there we are, talking about business. We talked about lines of credit, letters of credit, CDs, and checking accounts. I'm trying to sell him on meeting his banking needs, and I tell him about my attention to detail and how well I'm going to take care of him. The call was ending just as all the others had. Mr. C. was simply not going to buy. My time was up. I got up to leave and, for the first time, Mr. C. walked me to the door.

I took a few steps out of his office, stopped, opened my briefcase, and turned around. I said, "Mr. C., catch!" and I tossed him two baseballs autographed by all the Indianapolis Indians. I said, "These are for Travis and Cody," and I left.

The next day his secretary came by the bank and opened a $30,000 CD!

Dave had found his customer's Chicken Soup and as a result was able to have success where none of his predecessors had.

Now, as the CEO of Six String Leadership, Dave has taken this practice to a new level and is continually on the lookout for opportunities to make someone's day. "It's about finding those hot buttons that excite the heart of your customers and letting them know you are aware of them and that you care enough to go the extra mile to make them feel special," Dave explains.

Here's what Dave and companies catering to celebrities do to give their customers their chicken soup.

Take One: Ask

Take Two: Collect

Take Three: Just Start

Take Four: Imagine

Take Five: Look for Opportunities

Take Six: Remember and Refer

Take One: Ask

I've watched the subtle way Dave has of asking those around him about themselves. He has made an art of asking excellent questions. Because we all love to talk about ourselves, he is never at a loss for conversation. If you ever find yourself chatting with Dave, don't be surprised to find yourself talking about the following.

Favorites: Your favorite car, restaurant, musical group, store, and charity.

Firsts: Your first concert, car, kiss, childhood memory, and job.

Fun: Your hobbies, sports teams, movies, and more.

Family: Your parents, spouse, children, or pets.

Former times: Your alma mater, high school memories, and work history.

One effective way to get people to open up is to reveal a little bit about yourself first. A grocery store I occasionally shop in, Sweetbay Supermarket, has found an innovative way of getting its customers conversing with the checkout attendants. The attendants' name tags are also printed with the words "Ask me about." The clerks add words that identify something that interests them.

Personally, I just can't help myself. As the attendant is ringing up my grocery bill, I ask about whatever is on the name tags. Thus far, I've had conversations about music, video games, football, tattoos, and motorcycles. Inevitably, in the course of the conversation, I reveal a little bit about myself. If these store attendants want to strengthen their relationship with me, they could find a way to incorporate what I've told them into the conversation the next time I am in their line. More on how to apply that idea later in the section called Remember and Refer.

Take Two: Collect

Once he has extracted these tidbits of information, Dave stores them away for future use. He's made a habit of collecting seemingly unimportant information about his customers, family, and friends, so he can use it later to make their day.

For you, this goes beyond collecting data about your customers in terms of who they are as a group. The basics of customer service dictate that you know your customers in terms of geographic location, financial status, gender, and the like. Here, we're talking about collecting information about the person in front of you. Dave does it informally, but you can have a formal method of collecting the information as well.

Celebrity clients of XPACS are given an eight-page client profile questionnaire with 125 questions asking about everything from the temperature of bottled water they enjoy to how they like their steaks cooked. Of course, the process is personalized as well. Clients can fill the questionnaire out online, or they can meet an XPACS Concierge for drinks and discuss the questions. It's all about what works best for them.

As we discussed in the last chapter, the Celebrity Services Department at the Gaylord Opryland Hotel calls their expected guests, or their assistants, in order to fill out their personal profile. What do they enjoy? What are their hobbies? Favorite Music? Beverages? Do they have any allergies? Do they have pets?

They use this information to give guests their Chicken Soup. For instance, on the form I filled out I noted that I was an actress, a patron of the arts, and that I enjoyed immersing myself in local culture. I arrived at my suite to find a mandolin case filled with gifts including a CD of the musical *Always Patsy Kline*, a book about the Grand Ole Opry, and a few jars of barbeque sauce. Having mentioned my puppy, Snowball, there were treats for her and some Maltese-themed gifts. My favorite flowers—tulips—and my favorite escape—*People* magazine—were also on the table.

When the Gaylord Celebrity Services team read the profile of guest Caroline Proctor, they saw that she was an avid cyclist. She was treated to a personalized bike jersey, a heart rate monitor, and Power Bars for dessert, presented with a flourish. One of the team members accompanying Caroline is a guitarist. He was surprised with a denim jacket with the Gibson logo on the back and a trip to the Gibson store. There, he was given a private tour of the workshop where some of the instruments are made. (If you are a guitar enthusiast, you will know how well that went over.)

The Gaylord team continues to collect information informally once a celebrity guest arrives. For instance, while I was holding interviews with their staff one morning, I happened to mention that I loved blood oranges and that I hadn't been able to find them. They surprised me with one for dessert and someone snuck into my room and added three or four of them to my fruit bowl. They have trained themselves to think this way. As Caroline exclaimed, "They don't miss a thing!"

You can train yourself to think this way, as well. Find a way to collect information about your customers that works for you in your business. Make it systematic and habitual, and remember, this is about personal touch.

Celebrity Dish

When David Cassidy, a big Yankees fan, stayed at the Gaylord Opryland, he was disappointed that he would miss a game that was not broadcast on television. Scott Johnson, formerly of the Celebrity Services team, found a web site that was broadcasting the game and had it hooked up to the flat screen TV in David's room. He provided popcorn, nachos, hot dogs, and even a chocolate Yankee stadium. Scott believes that David was impressed.

Take Three: Just Start

It is action that separates red carpet service professionals from the rest of the pack. Many people talk and dream about what they'd like to do. Celebrity Experience providers take action to make it happen. In order to take action you just have to *start*. I was reminded of this the other day by none other than Dave Timmons himself.

Dave and I belong to a Mastermind group of five speakers, one of whom is Corporate Comedian David Glickman. Recently, we were all on a conference call where David told us that his son Howard, a six-year-old budding Steven Spielberg, had produced, directed, and starred in a short video that won him first place in his elementary school contest and then in the entire region. Howard's movie was on its way to the state competition.

As we congratulated David on his son's brilliance, I thought to myself, "I'm going to send Howard a note applauding his achievement." Great idea! Then I went on with my day, weeks went by, and while the note was always in the back of my mind, I never got around to writing it.

Cut to our next Mastermind meeting at the home of one of our group members where I'm listening to David Glickman tell us how over-the-top excited his son was to receive his very first fan letter. Who was it from? Of course, it was from Dave Timmons.

The difference between me and Dave in this situation? We both had a great idea that clearly would have (and did) make young Howard's day. Yet, for me it was just an idea that I would get to at some point. Dave, on the other hand, pulled out a note card while we were all on the telephone and wrote, "Dear Howard, Congratulations!"

I asked Dave what makes him such an action hero. "I know that if I just start the process as I get the idea that I will finish it. So I make it a habit to start right away, even if I don't have time to complete it right then."

Got an idea for giving your customers their chicken soup? Start now. Begin the letter, make the phone call, gather the materials—do whatever you need to do to get the ball rolling and you'll be an action hero, too.

Take Four: Imagine

When you start to incorporate the "Give 'Em Their Chicken Soup" philosophy into your daily routine, you will be amazed at how much fun it is for you. Often the giver has as much fun as, if not more than, the receiver. You'll find yourself really stretching your imagination to come up with bigger and better ways to make memories for the people you serve.

For instance, the Celebrity Services team at the Gaylord Opryland Hotel once welcomed a science teacher to Nashville. They knew he loved banana pudding. Did they just put a bowl of banana pudding in his room? Of course not. They filled a beaker with banana pudding. He was thrilled with the banana pudding, but even more excited when he saw it was presented in a beaker. When they discovered one of their guests worked at a paint company and loved chocolate chip cookies, what did they do? They partnered with their pastry team to make the cookies into the shape of paint cans. The brushes were made out of white chocolate with milk chocolate handles. The company logo was on the paint cans.

"My team loves to get creative, think outside of the box, and really tries to go to great lengths to discover what we can about our guests in order to delight and Wow them!" says Celebrity Services Director Pam Huff.

Put your imagination to work and see if you can think of inventive and memorable ways to give your customers their Chicken Soup.

Take Five: Look for Opportunities

The reason Dave Timmons is one of the best at giving people their Chicken Soup is that he has trained himself to constantly look for opportunities. As a result, he has a reputation for going out of his way to surprise his clients, friends, and family members in ways that make him unforgettable. While his motives are pure, his diligence in this habit does not go unrewarded. He creates a buzz wherever he goes, and business comes his way as a result.

For example, in 2004 he was speaking at an event in Indiana where he met a gentleman by the name of Dick Nye. Mr. Nye was the executive director for the Indiana Association of Realtors. He and Dave exchanged business cards and stayed in touch on a semiregular basis for the next couple of years about the possibility of Dave speaking at the annual leadership conference Mr. Nye's association held every January.

In 2005, the association chose a different speaker for the event, but Mr. Nye encouraged Dave to call back for the following year.

Then, one day, when Dave was in Bradford, Pennsylvania, heading toward the airport he passed a white, hand-painted sign that read "Nye's Tavern" and had an arrow pointing to a long dirt road. Remembering his prospective customer, and finding the sign amusing, Dave drove back around and took a photo of the sign. When he got home he sent the picture to Mr. Nye with a note that read, "Hey Dick, just wanted you to know that your family enterprise is going strong in Bradford, Pennsylvania."

Thirty days later, Dave was invited to speak for the Indiana Association of Realtors. "While I don't tie the engagement directly to that photo and note," says Dave, "I do know it made an impression. I found out later that Dick Nye was retiring. When he received my photo he forwarded it to his entire board with a note that read, 'Everyone has wanted to know what I'm going to do when I retire!' They all loved it!"

Again, their Chicken Soup is that special something that pertains only to them, and lets them know you're listening.

Celebrity Sighting

What works on the job can also work in your personal life. In a post on www.hellomynameisblog.com, Scott Ginsberg demonstrates how giving others their Chicken Soup can really spice up your social life.

As a single guy (by which I mean, not married), I've been on my share of dates. As a marketing guy, I've seen my share of unique ways to spread the word about ideas, products, and web sites. Now it's time to merge what I've learned.

1. *I was once introduced to a girl named Karen by a mutual friend. She and I clicked right away. We discussed sushi. She said she had always wanted to try it. I made a mental note. The following week I found out where she worked and stopped by her office with a little card, the front of which had a picture of a box of California Rolls. On the inside I simply wrote, "Sushi?" and left my business card. I handed it to the receptionist. By the time I returned home, there was an e-mail from Karen. She was ecstatic. We went out the next night and then dated for a few months.*

2. *I'm big on gifts. Nothing fancy, just something cute to start the first date off on the right foot. More important, something unique. Not flowers, candy, or a mixed tape. Something memorable. Now, I'd been talking to this particular girl for a few weeks. I knew that she loved (more than anything in the world) her soaps. One Life to Live, Days of Our Lives, all that stuff. So I stopped by Walgreen's to pick her up a copy of Soap Opera Digest. I wrapped it up and had it waiting on the seat of my car when she stepped in. She almost cried when she opened it and told everyone she knew about it.*

Great ideas, Scott! Turns out Chicken Soup isn't just for the workplace.

So, how can you start to get into the habit of seeking these kinds of opportunities? Whenever I speak to audiences about giving their customers The Celebrity Experience and we get to this point in the presentation, I give them the following assignment.

1. Choose *one* customer. Only one.
2. Have a conversation with the goal of finding out three things that you didn't know before. Don't make it a formal interview. Just have fun, ask questions that show interest, and see what you can find out.
3. Take action on the information you know. (In other words, find some way to Give 'Em Their Chicken Soup!)
4. Tell the story—share what you did with your coworkers and tell them about the reaction you got.
5. Pass it on—encourage your coworkers to do the same.
6. Repeat—with other customers.

Try this and I'll bet you find that customers are buzzing about you in no time. You'll be taking them from the level of strangers to friends, and people like doing business with their friends.

Celebrity Sighting

"My only regret is that I can no longer go camping with the Girl Scouts. Those days are over." When Activity Directors Wendy Nelsen and Tina Detweiler heard these words from Miriam, one of the elderly residents of Country Meadows, an assisted-living community in Hershey, Pennsylvania, they could have smiled and forgotten about it. Instead, they decided to delight her by proving her wrong. They made a phone call to a local Girl Scout leader and started planning. Miriam, who still had her original membership card from the 1930s, her beanie with badges, canteen, and handbook and could re-

cite the Girl Scout promise from memory, was treated to a night of camping—in the Activities Room!

The local troop set up tents and spent the night with Miriam and other residents of Country Meadows, singing songs, telling ghost stories, and eating s'mores!

Miriam's reaction? "She was thrilled," say Wendy and Tina. Of course she was. The activities directors had given Miriam her Chicken Soup.

Take Six: Remember and Refer

Perhaps your job doesn't lend itself to giving tangible gifts to your customers. That's okay. Sometimes Chicken Soup doesn't come in a tangible form but in knowing your customer and recognizing what's important to them.

Aren't you impressed when the server at your favorite restaurant remembers how you like your coffee? Don't you feel special when the bagger at your grocery store recalls the discussion you shared the last time you were there?

As Hollywood Producer Tisha Fein told me, "Celebrities love it when you notice things about them. If they've changed their look, I always comment and compliment them on it. Or I remember what we talked about the last time we met."

Celebrity Sighting

Wes Bard, CEO of Lutheran Home of Southbury in Connecticut, shared the following:

When we first moved to Connecticut, my wife and I spent a lot of time checking out different restaurants. We went to Carl Anthony's Trattoria in Monroe and liked the food and the *service, so when my brother visited from Pittsburgh we brought him there to eat. Three weeks later we went back and had the same waitress. She remembered every single thing we had ordered on that last visit. My wife and I decided right then and there, "This is the place we want to go." We get great service there and it feels like family. Because of that service I spend at least $5,000 in that restaurant every year.*

Pay attention to what your customers say when you are interacting with them. Do they have grandchildren? Are they going on vacation? Do they love peppermint ice cream? Remember these little details and refer to them the next time you see your customer. You'll be building a loyal fan base in no time.

Celebrity Sighting

When Corporate Comedian David Glickman was hired to speak for a group of 1,000 school cafeteria employees, he was told that about a third of the audience members did not speak English; they spoke Spanish! David does not speak Spanish; he speaks English. He was told not to worry about it and that those who did not understand him would still enjoy the music that is part of his programs.

This was not good enough for David. He took the time to learn the following in Spanish:

Hi. I'm David Glickman. Please allow me to apologize to you that I am not able to speak Spanish. I wish I could! I wrote this out and had a friend translate it for me, because you are a very important part of my audience and I wanted to talk to you, too. I wish I could speak Spanish, because we could really have some fun.

I could talk about all the people who work in the downtown office who only speak English. You know, the ones who send you all the recipes that make no sense. If I could speak Spanish, I could make fun of them and they'd have no idea what I'm saying about them. Wouldn't that be great? But, unfortunately, I don't speak Spanish, so I won't be able to say all those bad things about management without them knowing what I'm saying.

But even though I'm going to go back to speaking English now, I think you'll still enjoy the program. I will be playing some music later that everybody will enjoy, so you can look forward to that. Thank you.

As you can imagine, they were rolling in the aisles! With that one move, David let the Spanish-speaking people in the audience know that he cared enough about them to perform part of his show specifically for them.

Jack Canfield told me another story that he calls his favorite example of customer service. This story stars a friend of Jack's who went way above and beyond to give her husband his Chicken Soup. As Jack tells it:

My friend came up to me at a conference in New York. We were talking about ways to make your husband feel special.

Her husband's favorite college football team was Notre Dame, and his favorite coach was Lou Holtz. Lou also hired himself out as a speaker at $10,000 a day. So she called up Lou's office and said, "I'd like to hire you as a speaker." Then she said, "I want to tell you about the client. I'd like to hire you for a day, and the client is my husband." It was her husband's 50th birthday, and she wanted to get him a gift he would never forget, so she hired Lou Holtz to come to their house and knock on the door at 9:00 A.M. She asked him to go golfing with her husband, have lunch at the club, tell Notre Dame football stories, and bring him home.

On her husband's birthday the doorbell rang promptly at 9:00 A.M. She called, "Honey, there's someone at the door to see you." And there was Lou Holtz, the legendary former coach of the Notre Dame football team. The guy still talks about it to this day!

Remember, when you reach out to your customers like this, in unexpected ways that are personally meaningful to them, you create an experience that they will never forget. It is one of the quickest, most fun, and effective ways to give your customers The Celebrity Experience.

The Star of Your Show

IT'S NOT JUST on the red carpet or in fancy hotels that celebrities get treated differently. Everywhere they go, they are made to feel special, unique, and important. They live a glamorous life of private jets, over-the-top parties, and the best of everything. They are ushered to the best seats in a restaurant, given private access to special clothing collections, and, whether they want it or not, get more attention in one day than your average Joe gets in a lifetime. In Hollywood, along Hollywood Boulevard, there is a large sidewalk filled with inlaid bronze plaques shaped like stars, each one with the name of an actor, musician, director, or comedian. It's one of the most famous walkways in the world, and it's called The Hollywood Walk of Fame. Yet, you need only look at the racks next to the checkout counter at your supermarket to see celebrities. Their photos grace the covers of magazines everywhere. Fans clamor to talk to them, be with them, get their autographs, or have their photos taken with them. Especially in the United States, celebrities seem to belong to an elite club, and everyone around them bends over backward to make them feel important and special.

So, how do you create a consistent experience that makes your customers feel as though they are important and special and the star of your show?

Take a cue from an association of payroll professionals that has seen extraordinary growth because they have a leader who focuses on making their members feel special.

From the Back Room to Hollywood Glamour

As I began to talk to my friends and colleagues about the concept of The Celebrity Experience, several of them mentioned the customer service delivered by the American Payroll Association (APA). Curious, I investigated by surveying a few of its past presidents and members. At the end of each interview, I asked this question: "Knowing what you know from your experience at the APA, what advice would you give someone who was starting a business and wanted to give customers The Celebrity Experience?" Each one, independently, gave me the same answer: "Call Dan Maddux!"

When Dan Maddux took over as executive director of the APA in 1992, the organization was in financial crisis and was operating out of a rented office. Since then, the membership of the organization has tripled to 23,000, and the APA owns its own administration building and several state-of-the-art training facilities. The leaders of the APA will tell you the success is a direct result of Dan's vision and his unwavering commitment to, and focus on, serving the organization's members.

Dan recognized that payroll professionals were often stuck in a back room somewhere, receiving none of the glamour or financial rewards that their coworkers received. As Sue Daring, payroll director for ACS in Schaumburg, Illinois, tells it, "The profession of payroll is misunderstood and not valued because there has never been a graduate or undergraduate degree associated with it. The people who work in payroll have often been neglected by Corporate America." Dan Maddux made it his mission, and the mission of his association, to change that by providing training to enhance the skills of payroll professionals, by obtaining recognition in corporate America for the profession through public education, and by representing the payroll professionals on a federal, state, and local level.

Yet, it's more than that really. Says Dan, "When people come to us, they are often suffering from a lack of self-esteem. For instance, they don't know how to ask for a raise, and they don't know they are worth asking for a raise. It's our job to make them realize just how important and valuable they are." And it's working. With the help of the APA, many members who worked in back rooms making minimum wage are now working out front making six-figure salaries.

How do Dan and his team make their customers, the members of the APA, feel like the stars of the show? *By making each and every decision from the point of view of the customer.* One of Dan's favorite sayings is, "What's in it for our members?" For instance, as past APA President Michael Hall tells me, "Dan has always looked for other avenues to ensure the financial success of the association and to keep the costs of membership down. He knows that many of our members pay their dues out of their own pockets, and he does not want the membership to bear the cost of our growth. We've rarely raised our dues. Instead we invest in real estate." The American Payroll Association has two state-of-the-art training facilities in Las Vegas, Nevada, and San Antonio, Texas, and has headquarters in San Antonio, Washington, D.C., New York City, and Las Vegas. Tuition is also a primary source of income, while membership dues make up only 17 percent of the organization's annual revenue. Where does that revenue go? Right back into member benefits!

By lavishing them with the best of everything. Knowing that his members were not used to receiving the perks and privileges afforded to others, Dan decided from the beginning of his term to change that paradigm. Their convention, called the Annual Congress, is quite spectacular, full of pomp and circumstance. Held in the best hotels and convention centers, the Annual Congress boasts a lineup of the best speakers in the country. Past APA President Kathy Menda tells me, "It shows we're a first-class organization all the way. That he takes the time to think about it and gives members opportunities we wouldn't ordinarily have, makes us feel so special!" Celebrity guests have included Henry Winkler, Suzanne Sommers, David Cassidy (ah, my first love!), and others.

And they have fun! It's important to Dan and his team that their members have a memorable experience. "Some convention hosts spend money on chair covers," he tells me. "But if you're in a beautifully decorated room, and no one is laughing and having a good time, then something is missing. I spend more money on interactive characters that tie in with our theme than on décor. Décor doesn't last—but these characters are full of surprises."

And so is the APA Congress. They've had members come dressed in togas, or ready for safari, or in their pajamas for a big slumber party. Once, when they were at Opryland's amusement park in Nashville, Dan wanted to keep his group together, so he gave them all water pistols. "These people went nuts, running back and forth for hours to the bathroom filling up the pistols. Everyone was having such a great time."

Sue Daring tells me, "Many people are willing to pay their own way to come to this conference because they leave feeling revitalized. They feel appreciated. That's the way Dan has structured this organization. The whole idea of the APA is to applaud other people."

By giving them opportunities to shine. That's what the American Payroll Association is all about—taking people who have been unrecognized, unnoticed, and underpaid for most of their careers and giving them the skills they need to shine. Dan and the team at the APA go above and beyond what most associations will do. For example, as with many associations, the members of the APA are offered opportunities to speak at their Annual Congress. However, those who volunteer to speak are offered, at no cost to them, a full day of speaking school by world-class speaker and presentation coach Patricia Fripp. In addition, Fripp (as she is know to her fans) gives private coaching to the president and incoming president of the APA as well as the association's man or woman of the year. In this way, Dan ensures their confidence and their stellar success at the podium. And he makes them the stars of the show!

By creating wow moments, one member at a time. Every member I spoke to had a story to tell me about how Dan and his team are always thinking about them, and the random acts of joy they've performed to make the members feel special. Michael Hall told me about the time that Dan offered his wedding chapel facilities (a side business that Dan owns) for one of their board meetings. As a special treat, he brought in a minister and invited any board members who wanted to renew their vows to their spouses to do so. "This year my wife is coming with me, and after our board meeting we're going to renew our vows. Then Dan's treating us to a candlelit dinner! Who else would even think of that? But that's Dan Maddux." Kathy Menda told me about the time he flew her to London to work with the UK payroll association, the Institute of Payroll Professionals. "While we were there, he made sure that I got to do more than you'd ever think possible. Really, this is one of the ways he makes me feel special. I mean, we did our payroll association thing, and then we went on the train, we went to a play, we went to dinner, we went everywhere you'd want to go in London."

Each person I spoke to had a story like this. But I think my favorite APA Celebrity Experience story came from past President Sue Daring.

As you know, we have a membership of 23,000 individuals, and for most of us, becoming president is an unthinkable goal. We think of the presidents as some of the most sophisticated and savvy people in our organization, and becoming the person who takes over that office every year is outside many of our hopes and dreams.

Still, lo and behold, in the year 1998, I was granted the incredible honor of becoming president of the APA. My husband and my son came with me to watch me be sworn in at the Annual Congress.

Each year, the president gets a special room at the hotel, and I was aware of this. That year, when my husband and son and I arrived at the hotel, there was some sort of commotion as we began to check in. We really didn't know what it was about, but we followed the hotel staff member as he escorted us up to our room.

He opened the double doors, and we gasped! It was the most unbelievable suite of rooms we'd ever seen. I think we counted about 13 different rooms. One of them had a baby grand piano. There was an exercise room, and an incredibly beautiful table in the dining area. Six of the rooms were the most luxurious bathrooms—one even had a VCR and a television. We learned that the very wealthy don't really need to bend over when they shower because there were spigots everywhere.

The hotel employees told us that they don't generally rent this suite out. It is reserved for dignitaries of the highest order. They told us the names of several U.S. presidents who had stayed there.

Never, in the history of the APA, had the association president had a room quite as grand and luxurious as this one.

We had so much fun! We gave tours of our suite all weekend and had parties every night for anyone who wanted to attend.

Sometime during the conference I visited Dan's room. I noticed that his was also very nice but not nearly as wonderful as ours.

One morning, someone knocked on our door and delivered Dan Maddux's cleaning to our room. It was then we found out what really had happened. Our luxurious suite of rooms was actually intended for Dan. He saw it and asked that it be given to us, anonymously and quietly, because he thought it would make a very special occasion for my husband and me. He took the room that was meant for us. We never would have known if his laundry had not been delivered to our door.

And even though this may be an interesting story for your book, it's not by far the most wonderful or kindest thing I've seen Dan Maddux do.

Now, please remember the recipients of these random acts of lavishness are people who have spent most of their careers going unrecognized. These are not wealthy people who are living the jet-set life. Yet, the leadership of the APA has chosen to view them as people worthy of the best, and as a result, the American Payroll Association and its members have become a force to be reckoned with.

At this point, you might be thinking to yourself, "I don't have the resources to put my customers up in extravagant hotel rooms or take them on trips to London." It doesn't matter. You can start right now with what you have in your business to give your customers The Celebrity Experience by making them the stars of your show. There are some very simple things you can do that go a long way toward making others feel like stars. It begins with action!

Take One: Use Their Name and Be Glad They Came

Take Two: Shine the Spotlight on Your Customers

Take Three: Serve a Singular Customer

Take Four: Remember "And Then Some"

Take Five: Listen, Act, Respond

Take Six: Have Fun!

Take One: Use Their Name and Be Glad They Came

A sure-fire way to gain your customer's loyalty is to make them feel like a part of the group. Do this by knowing who they are and welcoming them into your place of business with open arms.

Use your customer's name. As we discussed in Chapter 2, "Red Carpet Arrivals," there is nothing that makes us feel as special as the sound of our own name. (Unless of course it's followed by our middle name, and called out by our parents when we're caught doing something we shouldn't. "Donna Lee Bouchard, come over here right this second!") But when we do repeated business with people and they call us by name, it gives us a feeling of being known and appreciated. One of the reasons I enjoy my current banking situation is that the drive-through tellers all know me by name. They even know the name of my dog, and have treats for Snowball whenever I come by. Occasionally, when I am forced to go to the drive-through at a different branch because of time or location restraints, I can't help but notice how impersonal it feels to have to give my driver's license as identification. At my regular branch, I am *known*.

Still, I'm the first to admit, remembering names isn't easy for everyone. Yet, if you make a commitment to giving The Celebrity Experience, it's a crucial part of the picture. By remembering your customers' names you prove yourself to be someone who cares enough to listen, and you begin to establish a connection between your customer and your company. For advice on how to remember names, I went back to Dave Timmons of Six String Leadership, who does this better than most people I know. Here are the five steps he gave me.

1. Make it important to you. Being forgetful about names is often a choice not a memory problem. I don't want to get too mushy here, but you have to *love* the human race. You have to want to show people that you care. Some people go an entire day without hearing their name once. The fact is, we light up when we hear our names. If you care about people, you ought to care about using their names, because every time you do you're going to be setting off something positive inside them.

2. Ask for the person's name a second time. Oftentimes we don't hear people's names the first time they tell us because we're busy thinking about the next thing we're going to say. When that happens to me, I'll just ask, "What was your name again?" It's that second time when you can really clear your mind and focus on what is said. Ask your new acquaintance to spell his name, or ask him where his name came from.

3. Repeat it. When you are first told someone's name, use it three or four times in the course of the conversation.

4. Make an association. If I just met you, I might say to myself, "Donna, Donna, Donna—Madonna." Then I might visualize a mole on your cheek, because it will help me remember Madonna when I see you. Then I'll remember your name is Donna.
5. Collect information. When you start putting bits of information together with a name, then it becomes a whole package. For instance, when I remember that you were born in Massachusetts and that your favorite color is red, it's easier to remember your name the next time I see you.

Aside from just remembering them, there are some fun ways you can use your customers' names as well. June Hussey, a public relations professional I had a scheduled call with, answered her phone, "Donna Cutting Fan Club." I loved it! The Stage Door Deli in New York City has been known to name its sandwiches after celebrities who frequent the restaurant. Could you name some of your products or services after your customers?

Renowned salesman and author Dale Carnegie once said, "A person's name is the sweetest and most important sound in any language." And using their names is the first step toward making people feel like they are part of the elite group of friends that is your business.

Show your customers you are glad they came. Is there anything worse than being made to feel as if you're imposing on employees because you want to do business with them? You've been there. The sighs, the rolling eyes, or even worse, the total lack of acknowledgment. Recently I was at a print shop hoping to have copies made. Granted the shop looked busy, but no one was standing in line at the copy counter. I walked up to the counter inches away from the sales clerk who was at the computer. She continued to work on the computer without acknowledging my presence. A few minutes later another clerk approached. "Ah," I thought, "now I'll be waited on." No such luck. Without even glancing in my direction, the second clerk held a conversation with the first clerk that lasted at least five minutes. Then she departed. I finally asked, "Is there a customer service representative here?" The girl at the counter slowly looked up and said, "Today is Lucy's day off." When I asked who was helping customers today, she scowled and said, "We are. We're busy."

I left and took my business to a different copy center.

Frankly, all that clerk would have had to do was look up, make eye contact with me, smile, and tell me she was assisting another customer. I would have gladly waited.

On the other hand, there is service like the kind I witnessed being delivered by a Southwest Airlines gate attendant at Tampa International Airport. As I waited at the airport gate to board my plane to Albuquerque, New Mexico, I watched the smiling gate attendant as she greeted several of the other waiting passengers. She was laughing and smiling the whole time, and seemed to really enjoy being there. As we stood in line to board, I noticed how she called many of the passengers by name as she took their boarding passes and wished them well on their way. She made upbeat, positive, and sometimes funny comments as they boarded the Jetway to the plane. When I reached her station, I told her I had been watching her and that she embodied that Southwest spirit I had heard so much about. She countered with, "Are you old enough to be traveling alone . . . or are you an unaccompanied minor?" Having just had my 40th birthday, I don't have to tell you she made *my* day!

Then again, Southwest Airlines is known for their Positively Outrageous Service. Attitude is the essential attribute they look for in each employee, and customer service is stressed from day one. To that end, everyone pitches in to fulfill the airline's customer promise of low fares, on-time flights, and fun to boot! I've even witnessed a copilot helping to load luggage onto the plane so we could leave on time. The company's mission statement reads: "Dedication to the highest quality of customer service delivered with a sense of warmth, friendliness, individual pride and Company Spirit." That spirit is what Southwest is famous for, with employees dressed in casual and colorful uniforms, joke-cracking flight attendants, and planes painted to look like killer whales. Chairman of the Board Herb Kelleher has been known to dress like Elvis, give out whiskey with airline tickets, and settle industry disputes by arm wrestling.

This kind of passion clearly works for Southwest. In 2006, the company recorded the lowest number of customer complaints of any airline—only 0.18 per 100,000 passengers. In 1988, Southwest was the first airline to win the Triple Crown Award for Best On-Time Record, Best Baggage Handling, and Fewest Customer Complaints. It went on to win the Triple Crown Award for five consecutive years. Southwest is the only U.S. carrier to be profitable every year since 1972. In 2006, it celebrated its 34th consecutive year of profitability, and after the September 11, 2001, terrorist attacks, Southwest was the only U.S. airline to make a profit that year.

Part of the company's secret is hiring people who are passionate about their work, like my newfound friend at the Tampa airport.

Her antics did not stop at the gate. Once we were in our seats, the attendant came on board and took control of the microphone. She led us all in a rousing chorus of "Happy Birthday" for a passenger who was celebrating her 80th birthday. The woman was presented with a bottle of champagne beautifully tied with a red ribbon. The gate attendant told jokes and sang funny songs into the microphone until it was time for the plane to leave. By the time we took off, passengers who might otherwise have had their nose in a book or been nervous about the flight were laughing, talking, and joking with each other.

The difference between the gate attendant and the sales clerk at the copy center is all about attitude. The sales clerk seemed bored, frustrated, and bothered by my presence and that of other customers. The gate attendant seemed like she was having fun! She was happy to be there, and happy to have us there, too. I find myself looking for her whenever I fly Southwest out of Tampa.

In order to give your customers The Celebrity Experience, you've got to treat each one as an honored guest. You've got to show your enthusiasm for your job and for your customers. And don't be afraid to have a little fun!

Are you and your team ready to take The Cheers Challenge?

Take Two: Shine the Spotlight on Your Customers

Take a look at your marketing materials, the building your business dwells in, and your practices. Are you honoring yourself, your interior decorator, or your customers? Here are a few ways you can shine the spotlight on your customers.

Use their photos. If hearing your name is the sweetest sound, then seeing your face is the sweetest sight. Take a look at how people will do anything to get noticed by Al Roker when standing outside NBC studios during the broadcasting of *The Today Show.* Why? Because they want to see themselves on television. Think about how you felt the first time you had your picture in the newspaper. Recognized? Noticed? Like you belonged?

One of the many things that impressed me about High Point University is that the dormitories and the student union were decorated with framed poster-size photos of HPU students. Instead of choosing traditional décor, they chose to celebrate their students. Perhaps you could honor your customers by finding creative ways to use their photos. For instance, speaker and author Sandy Geroux ends each of her programs with a PowerPoint montage of photographs of her audience members, and she sings a beautiful song while it plays. Her audience goes crazy with delight! We've all eaten in restaurants that line their walls with autographed pictures of celebrities. However, I ate in a restaurant in New Orleans once that hung framed, autographed photos of its regular customers. Who wouldn't want to come back again and again to see his smiling mug on the walls of your business?

Make it all about them. For example, the Kester International Promenade at High Point University is lined with the flags of the countries represented by the student body. If HPU welcomes a student from a country not yet represented, that student receives the honor of raising that country's flag.

When Dave Timmons was the VP of Consumer Banking for NationsBank, he hung the paintings of local artists on the walls of his bank. Again, who wouldn't want to do business with you, and bring friends along, when something he created was hanging on the walls?

Here's one of my favorite examples. Dedicated to the idea of giving back, the luxury real estate team from The Campins Company donates much in the way of time and money to charity. The difference between The Campins Company and others who do the same? Founder Katrina Campins and her team donate money in the names of their customers.

With a little creativity, and by putting the focus on *them*, you can easily make your customers the stars of your show!

Take Three: Serve a Singular Customer

This is the advice given to the staff and faculty of High Point University by President Nido Qubein. "We are in the business of creating a happy student. Singular, not plural. It is an individual experience." While it may be daunting to think about giving The Celebrity Experience to every one of your customers, it doesn't have to be. Start with the person in front of you right now. What can you do or say to make that individual feel special? What can you do for that one person to make the experience with you extraordinary? If you think this way about each customer who is in front of you or on the phone with you, you'll find that your random moments of specialness add up. Before you know it, everyone who does business with you will feel like the star of your show.

Take Four: Remember "And Then Some"

When I visited the campus of High Point University, one of the people I met was Roger Clodfelter, who holds the title of Director of WOW! I asked him about his job duties and he told me, "I ensure we deliver an exceptional experience to our students and guests—and then some." It's in that realm of "and then some" that you will find yourself giving a real Celebrity Experience. What does that mean for High Point University? It means many things, but here are a few of them that caught my attention. Every single day one of Roger's duties as Director of WOW! is to walk around campus and hand deliver cards to students celebrating a birthday. On Valentine's Day, Roger and University President Nido Qubein strolled the campus giving out half-pound candy bars to each person they met. And HPU students are no strangers to free food. On hot days you'll notice the ice cream truck dispensing frozen treats to students and guests at no charge. In the winter, it's hot chocolate or warm apple cider. Daily, student volunteers staff booths throughout the campus giving out snacks of all kinds. And as you walk the campus, you'll notice the upbeat music that is playing. "It's all intentional," Roger tells me.

"The décor, the water fountains, and the music serve to make it a light, fun, and energetic place to be. We want our students to mingle and feel good." To that end, they widened their campus walkways so students could walk side by side. If all that weren't enough, the leadership at HPU knew that although they have never had security issues on their campus, parents are always concerned with their children's safety away from home. So they offer free valet parking from 9 P.M. to 2 A.M. for any students who can't find parking spaces close to their dorm rooms. And wait . . . there's more! When President Qubein realized that construction on campus was causing dust to settle on students' cars, he decided to pay to have their cars washed once a week. Student activities groups are hired to do the work, and in doing so raise money for their clubs. Now that's the definition of "and then some." When I asked Roger Clodfelter what he loved about being the Director of WOW! he answered, "Every day I come to work and my job is an experiment." The only challenge? "How do we top ourselves?"

By the way, if you're wondering what the payoff is for all the free services given to students, here's what Vice President of Enrollment Andy Bills has to say:

The name of the game is to ensure that every student receives an extraordinary education in a fun environment with caring people [customer happiness] which leads to higher student retention rates [customer loyalty]. When you couple higher retention of existing students with increasing numbers in your freshman class, this directly impacts the university in a very positive way. Traditionally, HPU has a freshman retention rate of 72 percent. Last year 91 percent of the freshmen here in May returned for their sophomore year in August. This is a direct result of their excitement about the direction of the university and a measure of their happiness here as students. The strategy is working and it is a lot of fun to deliver a "Celebrity Experience" to our customers [students].

I guarantee you that whatever you are doing now, you can top yourself by remembering, "and then some." For instance, Diane Anderson of St. Petersburg, Florida, told me about her auto mechanic at Wilsey Auto Service, Inc. who goes the extra step of cleaning her car inside and out every time Diane brings the car in for service. When they are really pressed for time, they give Diane a coupon for a full-service car wash and detail. It starts with going that extra mile. What could you do for your customers as a courtesy that you aren't doing now? Washing her car takes some extra time, and it stands out to Diane because no other auto mechanic has ever offered such service. As a result, they have earned Diane's loyalty. Remember "and then some."

Here's another example that happened to me just recently. As I write this story, I am in Chicago preparing to speak for an association conference tomorrow. I arrived last night so I could spend a day in the hotel room writing this chapter. When I got off the plane, I rented a car to drive myself to the meeting location. Now, I've rented many cars in my years working as a professional speaker. Often I take a shuttle bus from the rental car counter to the car lot, and I encounter many different forms of customer service. Some drivers load my luggage into the shuttle bus, some don't. Some smile at me and welcome me aboard, some don't. Some drive carefully and considerately, some don't. The driver I met last night, however, did everything I had hoped for *and then some*. His name is Ken, and he is a driver for Alamo Rental Car out of Midway Airport in Chicago. He welcomed me on board with a warm smile and a friendly hello as he loaded my luggage into the shuttle bus. Usually this is where it stops. But as I rode, Ken told me everything I needed to know about Chicago.

He told me what the weather was at the time and what it would be three days later. He told me that the traffic is always the same—bad—and that I should always leave extra time to get anywhere. He told me how to get back to the rental car lot, and exactly where and how to return my car. He told me where I could purchase gas close to the lot. He told me about sights I might like to see in Chicago and the best places to dine. I didn't even have to ask him. (The true mark of a celebrity service professional: Answer all the questions your "celebrity" might have, and the ones they don't even know they have, before they ask.) When we arrived at the lot, he told me to stay in the shuttle bus, and he pulled my rental car around and loaded up my luggage. As I came out of the bus, he helped me inspect the car for damages. Never, in all of my travels, have I encountered such service by a shuttle bus driver. Ken has mastered the art of And Then Some.

Why just go through the motions when you can challenge yourself to be extraordinary . . . *and then some?*

Take Five: Listen, Respond, Act

If you want to impress upon your customers how important they are to you then listen to them. Listen to their stories and listen to their opinions. Actively solicit their feedback about your service. Then respond to the feedback, and take appropriate action. When some of the members of the American Payroll Association told Dan Maddux that with all the PR they had done to raise awareness about the profession, there was still a problem with the image of a payroll worker, Dan *listened.* He responded to their concern, and he acted. The result was the formation of National Payroll Week, which is held in September and celebrates the hard work by America's 156 million wage earners and the payroll professionals who pay them.

When students of HPU complained that there were not enough parking spaces in front of the registrar's office when they were trying to pay their bills, some of the faculty parking spaces were taken away and 15-minute parking was put in their stead. HPU has suggestion boxes all over the campus, encouraging students to offer other ways HPU can give them an extraordinary experience. The key to making suggestion boxes or any other listening device work is to respond and act on the suggestions. Of course, remember to give credit to those who make suggestions. HPU staff members follow up on student ideas immediately and each student is rewarded with a free trip to Starbucks just for making a suggestion.

John Wood, owner of Hub Plumbing & Mechanical, one of our Celebrity Experience Hall of Fame members, told me, "We follow up every plumbing call with a five-question survey. It's how we monitor our service. We call them 'Happy Calls.' Although most customers rave about our service, I love hearing the gripes. It's a challenge for me to see what I can do to turn the situation around. The question I ask is, 'What do I have to do to make this better for you?' " And if it's at all possible, he does it.

Ask questions of your customers, but don't ask the easy questions. Instead of "How did we do?" ask "What could we do better?" Their responses may be hard to hear at first, but by listening to the answers, responding positively, and acting on their suggestions, you will begin to understand how to give your customers The Celebrity Experience that will make you and your company look like stars.

Take Six: Have Fun!

Giving your customers The Celebrity Experience should be fun! It's not all white gloves and formal affairs. Let your hair down and create the kind of experience that will get people laughing with you. Comedic musician, Victor Borge, said, "Laughter is the shortest distance between two people." Shorten the distance between you and your customer by having some healthy fun. For the American Payroll Association it may mean water pistol fights and toga parties. For Pike Place Fish Market in Seattle, Washington, it means allowing customers to catch their fish as it's thrown to them. For Southwest Airlines it means flight attendants who crack jokes over the intercom, decorating its terminals for holidays, and planes painted in bright colors.

Ask yourself, are we having as much fun as we could be with our customers? What can we do that is unique to our situation that would make our customers feel as though we were one big, happy, laughing family?

Those are just a few of the ways you can create a customer service atmosphere that makes others feel important, special, and like the stars of your show. Before we move on to the next chapter, I'd like to share one last story of a service professional who went above and beyond to let one of his customers know he was a star.

As I was preparing to write this book, I received a letter from the father of my friend David Glickman.

Dear Donna,

My son, David, told me about the book you are presently writing and thought you might be interested in a positive and moving experience that I had several years ago in dealing with a roof repair company in Sarasota, Florida.

After a heavy rain and windstorm two years ago, I noticed a leak in the roof of my home. From the yellow pages I picked a roofer at random because the roofer I usually called was too busy to even return my calls. McAllister General Contractors sent a man to look over the job. I took him into my garage to show him some of the extra roof tiles I had in case he needed them. He noticed that my car had a special Florida license plate, starting with the letters DV, and he asked about it. I told him that the special DV tag was issued to disabled veterans.

Tom climbed onto the roof and came down shortly. We talked for a few moments, mainly about the war in Iraq. He told me he had a close relative serving there.

Now at this point, I have to give you a little background on myself. I am a WW2 veteran (79 years old at that time). While serving in the infantry in Germany in 1945, I was severely wounded, which resulted in the loss of my left arm and my left leg, below the knee. I do not use a prosthesis for the arm, but I do wear an artificial leg. On the day Tom came to look at the roof, I was wearing shorts and a T-shirt so my double amputation was quite obvious. We talked about war in general, and he asked if I had received my injuries in WW2. I told him I had but that I managed very well, and after 60 years of being a double amputee about the only thing I couldn't do was repair roofs! We both laughed and he left.

Two days later I saw the McAllister truck pull up to the house, and two men got out and climbed onto the roof. In 20 minutes they left and never even came to the door. I could see that they did repair the roof.

A day or so later I received the enclosed bill marked: Paid in full. Enclosed, also, is a copy of my thank-you note to McAllister Contractors. I hope this will be helpful and is what you were looking for. I was very touched by the whole experience.

Sincerely yours,

Lou Glickman (David's Dad)

And here is Lou's thank-you note.

To Tom Wilson and McAllister Management and Employees,

Today I received the invoice for roof repairs done at my home on Monday, April 25, 2005.

I'm not sure how to respond to such a beautiful, magnanimous, and unexpected gesture. This year, 2005, is exactly 60 years since I was wounded in Germany during WW2 resulting in the loss of one arm and one leg. In all those years no one has done what you have done to thank me for my service to our country by rendering a "Paid in Full" invoice for work done! I was truly moved by this.

So, I thank you for your heartfelt thoughtfulness and generosity.

Most Sincerely,

Lou Glickman

P.S. I just hope our citizens and government will be appreciative of our armed forces around the world who are presently serving all of us.

Star Power

WITH CELEBRITY COMES POWER. Lots of it. The higher your star continues to rise, the more people will listen to you. So-called A-list stars like Tom Cruise, Julia Roberts, and Will Smith, who can influence what movies you see based on their names alone, are given much more creative control over their projects, more money, and even back-end deals that give them a percentage of studio profits from the film. Although a celebrity such as Hilary Swank may have started her career living in her car, auditioning for anyone who would see her, and accepting $75.00 a day for starring in a movie (her reported paycheck for *Boys Don't Cry*), her Oscar win in 1999 changed everything. You can be sure she now has her choice of projects and a voice in her salary negotiations. Celebrities like Clint Eastwood have opportunities to participate in all aspects of their chosen career, sometimes producing, directing, and starring in the same movie.

With celebrity also comes influence. When Ellen De-Generes parodied a *Saturday Night Live* skit with a commercial for Aqua2Go, a product developed by entrepreneur Stacey Griffin, the results were immediate. That very day, Stacey's e-mail inbox was filled with orders, including one from a large supermarket chain. When Katie Couric showed us her colon on *The Today Show*, people ran to their doctors' offices for a screening. And just one positive word about a book from Oprah, and it becomes an immediate best seller. (Oprah, can you hear me?)

It's not just the A-list celebrities who have power and a persuasive effect on the world. Remember the *General Hospital* Luke-and-Laura craze of the eighties? There were actual newspaper reports of an increase in the number of newborn babies named Luke and Laura. For good or bad, people in the public eye influence the clothes we wear, the charities we support, the bodies we crave, and the opinions we hold.

Celebrities have choice, a voice, control, influence, and power. If you want to give your customers a true Celebrity Experience, then consider giving them more power and participatory control within your business. Inviting your customers to play a part in and influence the direction of your company will increase buy-in; as a result they will buy more from you.

Here's an example of an American institution that knows the power of customer engagement.

My Day at the Races

It's April 29, 2007, and I'm sitting next to NASCAR superstar Jeff Gordon as he whips around the track at the Talladega Superspeedway in Alabama, going 198 miles an hour. I listen in as Jeff communicates with his crew, and feel the thrill of being in the lead car. Next, I'm in the air, watching from above as Dale Earnhardt, Jr. races to what he hopes will be a win on what would have been his father's birthday. Then I'm next to Jimmie Johnson, just behind Jeff Gordon, as the checkered flag comes down and Gordon finishes first (with Jimmie and me a close second) for his record breaking 77th career win.

Okay, I'm really sitting on my couch in St. Petersburg, Florida, watching it all on television. *But it feels as if I'm right there*. This is because sitting next to me is my laptop computer, and I've logged into TrackPass Race View on NASCAR.com. It's like a video game, with 3-D effects, that allows fans to follow the race and their favorite drivers as if they are right there with them. You can select your favorite driver, or switch between them all, listening to the in-car audio feeds, watching their live position on the track, and noting their current speed and whether they are on the throttle or brake. You can watch the cars from an aerial view, from inside your favorite driver's vehicle, or from the front. NASCAR uses this technology to put fans "inside the helmet."

Founded in 1948 by Bill France, Sr., NASCAR's mission has always been to provide its fans with the ultimate sports entertainment experience. It does this by giving fans power in a way unlike any other professional sport. On the couch at home, fans have the power to feel as if they are right there in the car with their favorite driver through the use of TrackPass Race View. In the stands at the track, fans have the same power with a hand-held audiovisual scanner called NASCAR NEXTEL FanView™, which was named by *Time* magazine as one of 2006's most innovative new products. Fans with DirecTV have the power, through NASCAR HotPass, to follow up to five different drivers at the same time. Fans can listen to driver-crew conversations on their Nextel phone. Thanks to the help of cameras placed inside the cars, at strategic places around the track and the stadium, and in an overhead blimp, fans can watch the race from numerous vantage points. They can even download video highlights of the races from iTunes. NASCAR uses technology to offer fans a variety of ways to occupy an insider's seat at the races.

"From the early days of NASCAR, we have tried to create a great racing product that exceeds the fans' expectations," Andrew Giangola, director of business communications for NASCAR, tells me. "This is why we provide a level of access to our fans that is not matched in any other sport."

The access does not end with technology. NASCAR provides the only sports environment with an "open locker room" or, in this case, an open garage. Depending on their level of ticket, fans can watch the prerace activities of their favorite drivers in action through garage windows. At NASCAR races fans can even mingle with the drivers.

Says Andrew, "Our drivers are seen as accessible, authentic, and down-to-earth people. In earlier days, Richard Petty was known to stay in the parking lot until every fan had his autograph. We encourage all of our drivers to continue the tradition and be out there with the fans. You would never see that level of fan accessibility to the athletes in other sports as you do here at NASCAR. For us, it's all about the customer experience."

But wait, there's more! For instance, when the Kansas Speedway opened in 2001, fans were given an unprecedented amount of star power with the inclusion of a Fan Walk area in the infield so they can be up close and personal during prerace activities and inspection. At many of the top speedways, fans can even walk the track prior to the race. "Many bring black magic markers and put their own autographs directly on the speedway," Andrew tells me. Talk about star power!

Nowadays fans who attend the races can even choose whether they want to stick with the traditional burgers and beer, or enjoy sushi and white wine for lunch. For instance, the Phoenix International Raceway now offers the Octane Lounge, where fans get to sit six stories above the first turn, dine on fine food, and even enjoy massages. To the thrill of fans, NASCAR drivers have been known to visit the Octane as well. These changes are intended to ensure that NASCAR is keeping up with its growing fan base, which now represents all levels of income. According to its own studies, 43 percent of NASCAR fans earn over $50,000, and 15 percent earn between $70,000 and $100,000 annually.

Giving its fans star power gives NASCAR customers a true sense of belonging. Just the use of technology alone has had a tremendous impact on the numbers of fans, who are now experiencing the sport in every conceivable medium. Every week over 1.3 million fans watch NASCAR programming on ESPN and Speed. This is more than four times as many as in years prior to the use of interactive technology. More than 640,000 fans access NASCAR.com every week, and more than 100,000 fans watch the five channels of NASCAR HotPass on DirecTV each week.

Today NASCAR has over 75 million fans in the United States, representing about one-third of the adult population. Female fans make up 30 million of that number. NASCAR races often draw larger crowds than a Super Bowl, an NBA Finals game, and a World Series game combined—a point that surprised and interested me.

Perhaps more important to the sport's bottom line, NASCAR fans are three times as likely to purchase NASCAR sponsors' products and services than fans in other sports, making them the No. 1 sport in fan brand loyalty. Perhaps this is why more than 100 Fortune 500 companies invest in NASCAR as part of their branding strategy. Giving your customers star power and making them feel included breeds loyalty to you and all associated with you.

Next up for NASCAR fans is the new Infield Community on the NASCAR web site. Here, NASCAR.com will turn fans into stars, allowing them to create their own personalized pages, upload photos, and meet other like-minded fans. They will be able to create their own online "crews" based on their affiliations with drivers, teams, and tracks, and NASCAR.com will engage the crews in a variety of contests and challenges.

Oh, and speaking of turning fans into stars, if you happened to be in Richmond, Virginia, in early May 2007, perhaps you attended the Jim Stewart 400. "Did NASCAR name a race after Jimmy Stewart of *Harvey* fame?" you ask. No, not *Jimmy* Stewart. *Jim* Stewart, a fan from Houma, Louisiana, whose contest entry was chosen out of 15,000 to receive naming rights to the NASCAR Nextel Cup Series race at the Richmond International Raceway in May 2007. The contest was sponsored by Crown Royal, which asked fans to submit a video or written entry about an occasion worth toasting. Jim won for his video that recalled his days of fishing with his dad, who currently has some health challenges. Jim's name was printed on tickets and related merchandise as well as in the newspaper and television schedules. He was given the privilege of waving the green flag to start the race, being mentioned at every television commercial break on the Fox telecast, and heading to Victory Lane to present the check to the winner who, in this case, was Jimmie Johnson. (My man Jeff Gordon came in fourth.)

This was the first time in NASCAR history that a race was named for a fan. It certainly won't be the last. It fits right in with the NASCAR strategy to give its customers star power.

Here are some action steps you can take to give your customers star power, too!

Take One: Give Them the Power of Choice

Take Two: Give Them the Power of a Voice

Take Three: Give Them the Power of Influence

Take Four: Give Them the Power of Belonging to the Inner Circle

Take Five: Give Them the Power of Making a Difference

Take One: The Power of Choice

If you were a child in the 1970s, chances are if I began to sing "Hold the pickle . . ." you could easily complete the jingle with "hold the lettuce." At that time, the fast food corporation in question took the country by storm by promising us we could have our hamburger any way we wanted it.

The power of customer choice is still a draw in the twenty-first century. Consider that when you walk into your local Starbucks, you can get your latte in a variety of flavors, made with whole milk, nonfat milk, organic milk, or soy milk, and with or without whipped cream. Customers are flocking to shops where they build their own bear, build their own burrito, and even build their own BMW. When we ask the waiter in the restaurant to leave the butter off our vegetables and bring the salad dressing on the side, we like to hear, "No problem."

The next time your teenager brings his iPod to the dinner table, think about how the entire music industry has been revolutionized by the power of choice. In the past, if you wanted to hear a specific song by a favorite artist, you had to purchase a CD for $15 or $20. It could be that you really only wanted the one song, but you had to purchase the entire CD. (Of course, in my day we had 45s for that purpose. Remember those?)

Then teenagers began to download specific songs off the Internet through a service called Napster. Well, this sent the music industry into a tailspin because the artists and people who worked on the specific song were being cheated out of compensation for their intellectual property. Then along came the new Napster (and later, iTunes). It offers a subscription-based service that pays the artist, and enables your teenagers (or you, for that matter) to listen to over three million songs, download the ones they like, and build a complete song compilation of their choosing on their iPods. It's like the mix tape of the twenty-first century. And teenagers are spending *more* money on music now, because they can choose their favorite songs, than when they had to purchase an entire CD.

Oh, and have you discovered TiVo or one of the other digital video recording systems yet? I can't get enough of mine. Now my husband and I can choose what we want to watch, when we want to watch it. We've got weeks' worth of *Lost* and *Ugly Betty* recorded so we can sit together when we have time and have a marathon TV weekend. Even when we watch something in real time, we can choose to watch it all the way through or we can pause it whenever we like. No more waiting for commercials to get up and make a snack. We just hit pause and can hit the restroom, make a snack, even walk the dog, and come back at any time to pick up where we left off.

Today, we consumers aren't satisfied with having choices made for us. We want to be in control. We want the power of choice. How could you give your customers more choices? What if you gave them:

- A choice in pricing?
- A choice to browse and not buy?
- A choice of many ways to contact you?
- A choice in how they receive your services—online ordering? Delivery? In person? Via telephone?
- A choice in scheduling?
- A choice in where they'd like to sit?
- A choice in product selection?

Here's a unique concept in health care that has at its heart the principle of giving choices back to people who've had many of their choices taken away.

Founded by Dr. William Thomas and his wife, Judy Thomas, The Eden Alternative is a concept that is transforming the way we care for elders. While working with the frail elderly in nursing homes and assisted-living centers, Dr. Thomas discovered that no matter how much medicine he had in his medical bag, his patients were dying—of loneliness, boredom, and helplessness. He realized the institutional settings that we have built for our elders are not places that revolve around human habits or creating a world worth living in. He wanted to change that.

To that end, he created The Eden Alternative and The Green House Project, a name for community homes for elders centered on the Eden method. Central to The Eden Alternative are 10 principles, one of which is:

An Elder-centered community honors its Elders by de-emphasizing top-down bureaucratic authority, seeking instead to place the maximum possible decision-making authority into the hands of the Elders or into the hands of those closest to them.

In other words, elder care communities that are guided by The Eden Alternative or have a Green House Project home, give their senior residents back their power of choice.

For instance, in a typical assisted-living center, visitors come and go without much input from the residents. At a Green House Project home, visitors must call ahead to ask permission to stop by. Isn't that what you would expect of someone who wanted to visit you in your home?

A standard elder care home might have meals at a predetermined time, give the residents two choices, and dictate what they can and cannot eat depending on what is listed on their medical charts. At an Eden Alternative home, residents can eat whenever they are hungry, and are free to open the refrigerator and choose whatever they would like. They are educated on what is healthy for them, according to their doctor, but then can make their own decision as to whether or not to follow the recommended diet.

Decisions about what happens in the home are made in a circle, where each resident, family member, and care aide has a chance to speak without interruption. Once all of them have had a chance to be heard, they discuss what they've learned from one another and decide, together, how to proceed. This differs from the usual model where rules are made by administration and must be followed by the residents.

These guidelines and tools give the customer—in this case, the elder residents—back their decision-making power and help to create a warm environment where human beings love to live.

Take a look at your own company or organization. Where are you hoarding power? Where can you give your customers more freedom and choice? Answer those questions, and you may find yourself creating a place where your customers love to be.

Take Two: The Power of Voice

If there is nothing we like better than the sound of our own name, perhaps what we like second best is the sound of our own voice. We all have something to say, and as it becomes easier to make worldwide connections, there are more and more people available to listen. Some companies are harnessing the power of the Internet and other tools to give customers their own say, and as a result keep them connected to their business.

Here are just a few ways that consumers are being given a voice.

Blogs. Companies like Southwest Airlines and Jobing.com use blogs (or web logs) to have conversations with their customers. A blog is a web site that is updated frequently, by one or more persons within the company, offering a behind-the-scenes look at the organization, communicating information to customers, and providing tips and education that relate to the target audience. While there are risks to entering the blogosphere (once a comment is posted and people have read it, it can be difficult to take back), if done creatively and with intention, a blog can help cultivate a personality for your organization. You also have the choice to allow readers of your blog to leave comments at the end of each post. This is where giving your customers a voice comes in. Die-hard bloggers and die-hard fans can't resist sharing their thoughts and opinions, and they will give you insights as to what your customers are thinking, feeling, and needing.

Says Vicki Steere, of Jobing.com, "Since launching the blogs, our recruiters are seeing more informed and prepared job seekers come into the interview process. Great recruiting is about connections. It's about building professional networks and relationships which act to further the brand name and attract more of the right people to the company."

Consider using blogs to deepen your conversations with customers and employees.

Personal web sites and spin-off groups. Web sites like myspace.com and *Purple Cow* author Seth Godin's squidoo.com are giving everyone in the world an opportunity to have a Web presence and share personal thoughts, talents, and passions with the rest of the world. Through posting videos on YouTube.com, anyone can be a star, and some have become instant worldwide celebrities, such as inspirational comedian Judson Laipply whose video "Evolution of Dance" landed him on *Good Morning America*, *The Today Show*, and *The Ellen DeGeneres Show*. Some companies are taking a cue from these sites, enabling their customers to either personalize their web site experience or create their own web site to further the cause of the organization.

This kind of open forum is giving Americans an even stronger voice in the world of politics. While all candidates are now making use of Internet technology to gather support and give the American people a voice, the candidate who has most strongly taken the idea and run with it in this election cycle is Illinois Senator Barack Obama. As of this writing, Senator Obama is a presidential hopeful and a candidate in the Democratic primary. Obama has focused a great deal of effort on building a following on the Internet, making it a central part of his grass-roots campaign. His supporters can easily launch their own pages on www.mybarackobama.com, create their own communities of like-minded friends, plan local events, and raise money on his behalf.

Running with the slogan "This Campaign Is about You," Obama encourages every one of his supporters to donate to the cause, no matter what amount they can contribute. When it came time to report the money he raised during the first quarter of his campaign, he not only gave the dollar amount ($25 million) but the number of contributors (50,000), stressing the importance of everyone's voice. He raised more money on the Internet than any other primary candidate ($7 million), and many of those donations came in amounts of $50.00 or less. Through his Internet strategy, Obama has placed importance on everyone's contribution, regardless of how large or small, and his acknowledgment gave each supporter a way to feel part of the process.

The campaign web site is also used to give Americans a chance to share their stories and their opinions with the senator and on the Web. There are regular e-mails, as well as blog postings, sent to supporters that ask them to share their ideas on the site. For instance, people were asked to send personal stories of how foreign policy affected them, and then those stories were posted on the web site. It is just these kinds of invitations that engage people and make them feel part of the process. This engagement has helped endear Obama, who has been criticized for his lack of experience, to enough Americans that he is, as of this writing, considered a close second to Democratic front-runner Hillary Clinton. While the final outcome remains to be seen, it's clear that Obama's grassroots efforts and focus on giving his supporters a way to voice their opinions have helped in making him a strong contender in the primary election.

Could you use the Internet and new technologies more effectively to gather support for your company or cause? You might argue that it's only young people who truly invest their time in posting to blogs, developing personal web sites, and watching videos on YouTube. Maybe, maybe not. Regardless, who are your customers of the future? The very people who are immersed in all of the Internet technology we've been discussing.

Anywhere and everywhere. With or without Internet technology, there are many ways to give your customers a voice. Southwest Airlines invites customers to send their travel tips in to be featured in their in-flight publication, *Spirit* magazine. Some companies feature stories and anecdotes shared by their customers in their newsletters or marketing materials. And some companies, as in the case that follows, will even feature a real customer (not just actors who play one on TV) in their commercials.

Brenda Coates was on her way to work as the administrative assistant to Christopher Dudley, VP of community relations for High Point University, when all of a sudden someone driving the car behind her crashed into the back of her red Dodge Neon. No one was hurt, but the rear of her car was damaged, and she exchanged insurance information with the other driver. That same day, she called her own insurance company and was told by a seemingly uncaring representative, "Well, you can put a claim in if you want, but now your rates are going to go up." Then she called the other driver's insurance company, which happened to be GEICO. To hear Brenda tell the story, the difference in attitude was like night and day. "The GEICO representative I spoke to on the phone was very compassionate, and immediately arranged for my car to be fixed. They gave me a rental car to drive in the meantime, and when I came to pick up my car, I discovered that they had completely washed and waxed it for me. Right away I switched insurance companies and wrote to GEICO to tell them why I had decided to sign with them." Well, the people at GEICO were so pleased with Brenda's letter, that they passed it on to Warren Buffett, who owns the company. He wrote Brenda a personal letter, thanking her, which she treasures to this day.

The story does not end with Warren Buffett's letter, however. A few months later, GEICO flew three of its senior executives down to North Carolina, from Washington D.C., to visit with Brenda. During that visit, they asked Brenda if she would like to film a television commercial for the company. Brenda agreed, and that is where her star treatment really began.

My daughter, Jennie, and I were flown first class to California, and when we arrived in Los Angeles, our chauffeur was waiting. Since it was our first visit to the state, he gave us a wonderful tour of the area as we made our way to Santa Monica. We stayed in a hotel where many Hollywood celebrities stay. GEICO even gave us spending money to use while we were there. The next morning, our chauffeur drove us to Hollywood to film the commercial. When I arrived on the set, I discovered that I had my own trailer with my name on the door, and a hairdresser and makeup artist were waiting for me. They had even assigned me my own personal assistant who was there to get me drinks, and do whatever I needed.

Brenda was filming the commercial with Burt Bacharach, who she said, "has a star quality about him. He just glided on to the set. He was also very sweet, and kept telling me how great I was doing." Brenda told her story into the camera, as Burt Bacharach retold it with his own music and funny lyrics. You probably saw the commercial. It was wonderfully creative, and I think Brenda has her own star quality about her! The commercial also gave a voice to the person who makes all the difference—the customer. My guess is that Brenda will remain a GEICO customer for a very long time. She has a sense of connection to the company, and now she has another GEICO story to share with family, friends, and visitors (like me) to High Point University.

Give your customers a place to tell their stories, and voice their thoughts and opinions, and you'll be creating a connection to your business that will keep them buzzing about your business and coming back for more.

Take Three: The Power of Influence

To witness the effect of consumer engagement, just take a look at the cultural phenomenon *American Idol*. This show transformed the reality show experience, inviting viewers to vote for their favorite contestant and giving them complete control over who stays and who goes. After the 2006 finale, viewers cast more than 63 million votes, apparently more than in the previous presidential election. Viewers are also given opportunities on the *Idol* web site to post to blogs, create photo albums, contribute recaps of the show, ask questions of the contestants, and make friends with other fans across the country. The in-studio audience members are encouraged to bring signs in support of their favorites, and give nicknames to contestants (Chicken Little Kevin Covais) or their fan clubs (Soul Patrol for Taylor Hicks fans). *American Idol* has given the power to the people and, as a result, not only has it consistently been at the top of the Nielsen

Ratings every season for the past six years, but in spite of DVR systems, this is one show viewers watch as it airs because they want to vote afterward. Hence, they aren't zipping through the commercials, and the sponsors are *very* happy.

Could you give your customers the same kind of influence over your products and services that *American Idol* gives to fans over the fate of its contestants? For instance, log onto www .innovatewithkraft.com, and you'll find that Kraft Foods is proactively seeking ideas for new products and packaging ideas from its customers. Microsoft uses its Knowledgebase, a series of articles written by users for users, to give customers a voice and to gain insights from customers that help the company to improve existing software or innovate new products. You may remember when M&Ms maker Mars Inc. invited customers to vote on which color would replace the tan. The creators of the television show *The Family Guy* had one episode that was entirely based on ideas that viewers had sent in for consideration.

I, myself, have felt as if I was given star power when Ben & Jerry's Ice Cream used one of my ideas. When I was being religious about sticking to my no-sugar, no-white-flour diet (an effort I have long since abandoned), I was seriously yearning for some Chubby Hubby ice cream. I wrote to the company requesting that they make a sugar-free version of their product. Was I surprised when a year or so later, they sent me a letter thanking me for my idea and letting me know the product was on the shelves. I even got a coupon for a free pint! Okay, they waited until many customers had suggested the same thing, and the letter was not personalized to me, but still, I felt the power.

Today, you can join Ben & Jerry's Chunk Spelunker group, which will give you insider information about new flavors that are coming out, special invitations to events at the scoop shops, and entry into special contests and giveaways. A few selected members will have the opportunity to be Honorary Flavor Cultivators and help the company come up with new fantastical creations. Hmmm. The Cele-berry Experience, anyone?

You can invite customers to help you cocreate your products and services by hosting focus groups, test-marketing your product with a small target audience, soliciting feedback through online surveys, or even using old-fashioned suggestion boxes. If you decide to write a blog, and you open your blog up to comments, you can even use those comments to find out more about what your customers are looking for and then provide it for them. Remember, though, to give credit where credit is due! Let your customers know that by doing business with you, they have star power.

Take Four: The Power of Belonging to the Inner Circle

Have you seen *The Ellen DeGeneres Show*? If you haven't, check it out for a great example of making customers feel like they are part of something special—that they are in on things. Ellen starts each show with a comedy monologue that typically reflects something that happened to her recently. She ends the comedy bit by dancing with her audience, who have been practicing for hours prior to the show.

While, like most daytime talk show hosts, she does welcome celebrity guests, she is also a master at making her audience members (those in the studio and those at home) feel like stars. Some of her guests include talented children, pets, and real people with extraordinary stories. Viewers are invited to send in photos of themselves, their pets, and their children. Ellen will often read a letter from a viewer on the air, and then surprise the letter writer with a telephone call in the middle of the show. When Ellen was hosting the Academy Awards, she kept her audience in the loop every step of the way. And one time, on a lark, Ellen gave out a telephone number so viewers could call the studio. There were so many calls it overloaded the network's phone system and shut it down for the rest of the day. Since then, show producers have set up a special phone line just so people can call in and leave messages for the show's host.

Ellen has made stars of her audience, and they feel as if she is their friend and they are part of her inner circle. The formula works! The show does consistently well in the ratings and has won Emmy Awards every season since it began.

You can learn from Ellen's example to make your customers feel as if they are in on things and a part of something special by being connected to your business. NASCAR does this brilliantly by giving fans opportunities to mingle with the drivers and have up-close-and-personal experiences with the speedway operations. Southwest Airlines even has a reality show that gives its customers a real insider's view into the airline industry—warts and all.

Let your customers into your inner circle by giving them a place to belong—a place that feels like theirs. A place where they can hang with their peeps! You can do this by personalizing the customer experience, hosting special customer events, or starting customer clubs and organizations.

For instance:

- Home Depot holds clinics where customers can learn how to complete do-it-yourself projects, which of course keeps them buying their supplies right in the store.
- Chellie Campbell, author of *The Wealthy Spirit* and *From Zero to Zillionaire* offers her readers the chance to join her "Dolphin Club." Through this online community you can connect with other Chellie fans, promote your own business, receive oodles of free goodies, and special opportunities.

- Wilson Creek Winery and Vineyards is host to several wine clubs that give members special invitations to elegant dinners, cruises, outdoor barbecues, concerts, wine tastings, and more.

For the customers of these organizations, it's the power of affiliation that magnetizes them—and a chance to mingle with their own.

This can work for any organization. Author Sam Horn told me that once, when she and her son were on a ski trip in Big Bear, California, they got snowed in and spent a few days hanging out at a neighborhood general store. All the locals who came in had their own personalized mugs at the store to drink their coffee from. As they took things from the shelves, they would pull "their files" out of a little shoe box, and add up their purchases, listing them on the slip of paper to be paid at the end of the month. It was clearly a place where the regulars had a sense of power.

Celebrity Sighting

Wes Bard of Connecticut shares that his favorite restaurant, Carl Anthony's Trattoria, is closed on Mondays. Each year, on one of those Mondays, the restaurant invites its regular customers (and it has many) to come in for a special dinner. There is a band, an open bar, and a beautiful buffet of food—at no charge. Customers feel as if they are part of an elite group of people. Says Wes, "Some of the servers even call my wife and me 'Mom and Dad.'"

Sometimes making customers feel as if they are inside the inner circle is a matter of personalizing their service. Terri Kabachnick is the CEO and founder of The Kabachnick Group, a consulting organization to the retail industry and the author of *I Quit, But Forgot to Tell You.* In the mid-seventies to early eighties she was the CEO of a retail department store in Connecticut. Terri had over 100 employees and their entire focus was on delivering customer service "like people had never seen" at that time. To that end, she called her employees STAR Performers and developed what she called Simplify Your Life Concepts. All STAR Performers were to behave as if they were personal consultants to their customers. Terri set aside a private facility, where customers would receive white robes to wear and be served refreshments while they were asked about their jobs, their likes and dislikes, and the images they wanted to project. STAR Performers would take the customers' measurements and perform skin analyses and color drapings. When next they returned, a specially designed room had been turned into their own personal closet. They chose from clothes that were in their perfect size and tailored to their preferences, with accessories to match. This personalized service raised the average sale by 10 times the usual amount.

Terri and her idea were written up in *Women's Wear Daily*, and she began to get requests from other retailers that wanted to learn to provide similar services. Until she started The Kabachnick Group, Terri was franchising the concept to retailers all over the United States.

You might be thinking—haven't I heard of this before? Yes you have. Saks Fifth Avenue has what they call their "Fifth Avenue Club." Recently, Terri was introduced by a leader within Saks as "the woman we took that idea from." Terri doesn't mind. Like me, she believes everyone should have a Celebrity Experience.

Take Five: Give Them the Power of Making a Difference

My husband and I were on vacation, in the charming town of Lititz, Pennsylvania, looking for a place to have lunch. Suddenly the smell of chocolate was in the air. We followed our noses, and there, in the window of a shop across the street and we spied a large fountain with chocolate pouring from its spouts. We thought to ourselves, "Life's short! Why not have dessert first?" No need, however. The tantalizing sights and scents were coming from Café Chocolate of Lititz, a quaint little shop that fits right in on Main Street in this enchanting little neighborhood. Here you can have lunch with a twist. Try Chili Con Chocolate, salad with chocolate vinaigrette, and dark chocolate truffles for dessert. It's a chocolate lover's heaven!

It's clear from the moment you walk into Café Chocolate that those who happen upon it could easily become addicted— not just to the chocolate, but to the friendly servers, the delightful ambiance, and the delicious breakfast and lunch dishes. It's also immediately clear that by patronizing the cafe you have power—the power to give back and make a difference in the community. And what could be more of a Celebrity Experience than giving back to the community?

Selina Man, the owner of Café Chocolate, worked on Wall Street for over 10 years until she, in her own words, "said yes to a midlife crisis." This turning point led her to become the chief operating officer for Ten Thousand Villages, an organization that markets and sells the handicrafts of artisans who live in developing countries. Selina continued her journey of giving back to the community when she left the organization to open Café Chocolate. The mission of the cafe is "Chocolate for Life!" Says Selina, "Of course, we can't live without chocolate! But we also sell chocolate for the lives of the people who grow it. Eighty-five percent of the world's chocolate is grown by six million small farmers in the rain forests of Africa, Indonesia, and Central America. When our customers buy our products they are helping to save the rain forest and support these farmers. We try to have our customers be a part of our mission to make a difference in the lives of those who grow our product."

Selina and her team let everyone know that at Café Chocolate they "Think Globally and Buy Locally"—supporting the rain forest and the small businesses of their local community. They cover their walls with nontoxic paint and cook using alternative energy. And instead of using traditional advertising, Selina reserves that portion of her budget to support the welfare of children and literacy through the local library. At the cafe they sell products such as T-shirts made in a factory in the United States that doesn't use sweatshops, and greeting cards that support the locals in a small fishing village in Maine. A portion of all her earnings goes to www.small-change.org, an organization that contributes to hunger relief.

While Selina and the team at Café Chocolate are working from their own sense of mission, they also give their customers a sense of power. When patrons dine at their cafe, or purchase a gift of food or goods, they know in no uncertain terms that they have just made a difference in the lives of others. Of course, the fact that the food is delicious doesn't hurt. But Selina knows she has a large core of like-minded customers who vote with their money by coming often to dine at Café Chocolate. These regulars are part of the reason why the two-year-old cafe was cash-flow-even within two months of opening, while most in the business don't break even for at least nine months.

Of course, there are several ways you can give your customers the power to give back. By simply aligning yourself with a cause you and your team are passionate about, you give your customers the opportunity to make a difference when they do business with you. Katrina Campins of The Campins Company, a luxury real estate company, brings her passion for giving back to the community to her business. She and the rest of her team regularly volunteer money and time for a variety of causes, including the Leukemia & Lymphoma Society. The Campins Company often donates money to the charities their customers support— in the names of those customers.

At High Point University, servant leadership is a top priority. HPU students donate approximately 27,000 hours of community service annually. For instance, students in the President's seminar on Life Skills put learning into action by service to more than 150 community agencies in High Point and the surrounding areas. HPU is also among the nation's first universities to be awarded a student chapter of Habitat for Humanity.

By giving your customers choice, voice, and influence, and by making them part of your inner circle and the way you give back, you engage them in a way that keeps them connected to you and your business. Consider how you might give your customers more power to cocreate your company, and you may find you've got customers for life.

6

Are You Anybody?

What not-so-recognizable actor at a movie premiere or member of a celebrity's entourage hasn't heard those dreaded words: "Are you anybody?" These are the people who become invisible next to the intriguing, glamorous, and charismatic celebrity whom everyone wants to meet, touch, and befriend.

Ethan, an assistant to a very famous, Academy Award-winning movie star (who asked to remain anonymous) told me about the experiences he has had with some of the personnel in the shops on Rodeo Drive in Los Angeles, California. On a typical day, working for his celebrity boss, Ethan is dressed in his blue jeans with a baseball cap and generally looking very casual. "I walk into the store and they won't even give me the time of day. Then, they find out who I work for and they can't do enough for me. They're offering me coffee, a comfortable chair, bringing out samples, and basically fawning all over me."

Gena Pitts can relate. Gena is a creative, vivacious, funny, and fabulous woman. She also happens to be the wife of Mike Pitts, former defensive lineman for the Philadelphia Eagles,

Atlanta Falcons, and New England Patriots. Here's what she has to say about the Are You Anybody Syndrome.

> People who market their services to celebrities will literally stalk them. They will do anything and everything to get their material in the hands of the athletes. What they don't realize is that those things go right in the trash. There is someone else making the household decisions, and that is the wife of the athlete. The wives are the household managers, and still salespeople will look right past us or shove their trinkets in our hands and briskly demand that we give them to our husbands.

Recognizing that she wasn't alone in this experience, Gena developed an entire business based on the idea that even the noncelebrity members of the household should receive the star treatment.

Silent Partners No Longer

Gena is the founder, publisher, and editor in chief of *Professional Sports Wives*, a publication and organization designed to give acknowledgment, support, assistance, and applause to the people she refers to as "the silent partners"—wives of professional athletes. She hears from readers of her magazine on a daily basis who are so grateful to have found someone who understands what it's like to be the silent partner of a celebrity, and watch that high-profile husband get all the attention and applause. On the phone with Gena, I told her that I considered her to be a celebrity as well. She laughed.

> The celebrity thing is too funny! You are one of only a few people to ever say that to me. I remember one time someone asked Mike for his autograph. I was standing next to him,

you know, as the wife, and was very proud. Suddenly, the person turned to me and asked, "Can I have your autograph, too?" "Me?" I asked. "You're asking *me* for *my* autograph?" I was so honored and excited that I was practically bawling. It was just nice to be appreciated and thought of so highly. I was used to being the person who stands to the side, and this person asked me for my autograph. I was so overjoyed, I couldn't stand myself.

So now Gena has embarked on a mission to remind the silent partners that they, too, are stars! In addition to the magazine, which provides marriage and family advice, tips for relocation, feature articles about the wives of athletes, and resources for the partner who actually runs the family corporation, the Professional Sports Wives association gives its members educational, social and professional networking opportunities, a bank of resources, and an opportunity to give back through charitable endeavors. Gena has also launched Professional Sports Wives Day, recognized by *Chase's Calendar of Events*, on which awards are given for the Mentors of the Year, Entrepreneurs of the Year, Philanthropist of the Year, and others. When it comes to Gena's business, the wife is the star of the show!

That's not to say that Gena doesn't still run up against the Are You Anybody Syndrome.

Just last week someone called the magazine wanting to talk to Mike Pitts. Now, Mike is the editor at large, but once I realized what the caller needed, I knew the person to speak with was Angela Shipp, our managing editor. But the caller was determined to talk to Mike and was really rude about it. It was like a cat and mouse game. I kept offering to transfer the caller to Angela, and he kept insisting on talking to Mike. I finally told him to just send his material, which will probably end up in the trash. I don't think the caller realized he was speaking with the publisher and editorial director of the magazine!

Unfortunately, Gena's experiences are not uncommon in the world outside of celebrity either. Too often, salespeople or service personnel fall all over themselves for certain customers, and dismiss others, however subtly, whom they deem as unimportant to their business. Gena has created an entire business to support and recognize people who are behind the scenes and unfairly receive the Are You Anybody? treatment on a regular basis. However, you can ensure that regardless of who you perceive them to be, everyone who walks through your company door receives the same respect as your best-paying customer. All it takes is a little action!

Take One: Delight the One in Front of You

Take Two: Assume That Everyone Is Your Best Customer

Take Three: Acknowledge Each Person in the Group

Take Four: Provide for the Entourage

Take Five: Train Your Team Well

Take One: Delight the One in Front of You

Recently, I asked my office manager, Rachel Street, to call a number of public relations companies to gather information for me. Based upon the information she received, I intended to ask two or three of them to send me proposals to handle the publicity for this book. One of the owners of the firms that Rachel called refused to speak to her. The owner's assistant kept going back and forth to her boss, relaying Rachel's questions and coming back with the reply, "She'd be happy to speak to *Donna* about that." Needless to say, she'll never have a chance to speak to me. We crossed her off the list of potentials.

On the other hand, the representative of a different firm treated Rachel as if she were the client, returning her call promptly, thoroughly answering her questions, and establishing a warm and friendly relationship with her. We offered this public relations professional the opportunity to send a proposal and are, as of this writing, seriously considering working with her firm.

Regardless who the "celebrity" or "important" client is who you are trying to land or impress, the people around them deserve the same level of respect that you are giving the other person. Ask the assistants or the spouses of a celebrity or CEO, and they will bombard you with stories of how they have been treated rudely or, worse, ignored while the boss or partner is fawned over.

On the other hand, when Sandy Geroux of the Geroux Performance Group was the vice president of programming for a local professional association to which she belonged, she regularly dealt with the assistants of speakers whom the group was flying in for its meetings. When the meeting was over, she would send a thank-you note to the speaker, and also to the assistant. "You wouldn't believe the reception those notes received!" says Sandy. "Most of the assistants told me it was the first thank-you note that had ever been addressed to them personally, even though they do most of the behind-the-scenes work."

While you don't want to go overboard and come across as though you are insincerely flattering the gatekeeper just to get to your target client, you do want to remember that often the way you treat your customers' assistants and spouses will get back to them. What's more, it's simply about having respect for the person in front of you. You know that your Red Carpet Customer Service is authentic when you, as well as everyone on your team, make an effort to delight each person who walks through your door.

Take Two: Assume That Everyone Is Your Best Customer

Much has been written about the importance of first impressions. More than likely, you and your team have attended training sessions about making a good first impression on your customers. Yet, have you thought about the first impressions you have *about* your customer? Have you ever looked at potential customers and decided by the way they dressed, spoke, or behaved or by their age, gender, or ethnicity how much money they would have to spend on your products and services, and proceeded to treat them accordingly?

Consider the following story by Liz Strauss, professional writer and author of www.successful-blog.com. This is from her April 18, 2006, post entitled, "Do You Know a Customer When You See One?"

I was in my mid-twenties. I had left teaching and had an executive job in downtown Chicago. I was a young professional with a disposable income, who needed some business suits. My mother had taught me the value of investment dressing—now that I'd finally quit growing. She had said it was worth buying classic, expensive clothing that fit well, because the investment never went out of fashion. A 36-inch inseam meant off-the-rack clothing wasn't an option for me, anyway.

It was a Saturday afternoon when I arrived at the storefront on Wabash Avenue. This was the kind of place where CEOs sat on embroidered couches reading *Forbes* magazine, while a wife or current affair of the heart decided which seven or eight suits and dresses she simply could not live without. Then he paid, and they both left happy.

Three women, all at least 10 years older than my mother who was 30 years older than me, were standing at the elegant counter when I walked in. I was wearing my baby blue down-filled ski jacket with the torn pocket, a bright red ski sweater with a bicycle tire embroidered on the front, and my blue jeans that came complete with frayed bell bottoms, a patch on each back pocket—have a good day/have a nice night—and a drawing in ink up the inside right thigh that I had made while talking on the phone the night before.

All three ladies, who worked on commission, looked up when I came in. I was the only other person in the store.

I wasn't the usual vision that walked through the door.

Two of the ladies—hoity-toity is the only word to describe them—frowned and immediately went back to talking. They had tried to intimidate me right out the door. It was sort of like that scene in the movie *Pretty Woman*. That didn't bother me. I was a saloonkeeper's daughter. Obviously they'd never seen one of me.

The third lady, who probably was there to make a living, came over as if I were a customer. We talked for five minutes. I went to a fitting room. She brought me six suits. I bought three of them. She made a $1,000 sale in a half hour. I so enjoyed the looks on the faces of Hoity and Toity as my new friend, Mary, rang up the sale, and we spoke of when I'd be back again. I said a cheerful good-bye to all three—Mary and the two with their jaws at their knees.

Mary became my personal shopper. I returned to that shop every two or three months for about five years. I tried to wear those same blue jeans whenever I went there. Just for the fun of it. Naturally, I updated the artwork each time for the occasion.

This story is not a unique one. I've heard several versions of the story about a wealthy man who dressed in raggedy clothing and was turned away at several car dealerships, but dropped 50 grand at the dealership where they treated him as a viable customer. Joe Wood, a technician for Hub Plumbing, told me, "My policy is to treat every potential customer with the same respect, using the same procedure, regardless of who I might perceive them to be. Some of my best customers have been brushed off by other plumbers because of the neighborhood they live in or the condition of their home. You can't always judge a book by its cover."

How many profitable relationships could you be leaving on the table because you've dismissed someone as a potential customer? Remember, that pimply-faced teenager you've been ignoring could turn out to be the next Bill Gates.

And it's not even about that, really. It's about respect. It's about being authentic with your customer service. It's about genuinely liking people and wanting to serve them. What level of respect would you give Tom Hanks or Catherine Zeta Jones if they walked into your place of business right now? I'm not talking about perks or special treatment—just respect. Everyone you serve within the context of your business deserves to receive that same kind of respect. As Marilyn Monroe once said, "Everyone's a star, and we all deserve to twinkle."

Take Three: Acknowledge Everyone

Ever been in a room full of people and felt invisible? Sure, we all have at one point or another. And it doesn't feel good. You can ensure that no customer who walks through your door ever feels like this by simply acknowledging each person in the party. This includes children, senior citizens, disabled persons, and others who often get overlooked in many situations.

Says elementary school teacher Carol Marion-Smith, "When I am talking with a service provider for an extended period of time, I really appreciate when they speak to the child who is with me as well. Oftentimes I have an entire conversation with someone, and they don't even acknowledge that the child is standing right there."

Barnes Boffey, director of Camp Lanakila in Fairlee, Vermont, says, "It's about speaking to the child like a human being—who they are. It's about role involvement with your job versus personal involvement. In my case, I know that parents are sending us their most prized possession, and they want to know that we have a personal connection with their child. So I make it a point to greet each child by name and ask them how they're doing. Then, everyone feels good about the interaction."

You can ensure that everyone feels welcome at your place of business with a simple warm smile and friendly hello to each and every member of a party.

Take Four: Provide for the Entourage

If you *really* want to give your customer The Celebrity Experience, then you will make provisions for others who travel with them. Hollywood stars come with an entourage. As producer Tisha Fein told me, "Celebrities come with their makeup artists, their publicists, their dancers, their musical directors, their tour managers, their agents, and their hangers-on." And because of their association with the celebrity, they, too, are used to getting some star treatment themselves. Why, even celebrity pets are pampered and have been known to go to the spa, take therapeutic swim lessons, drink water from large champagne glasses, wear diamond-studded collars, have acupuncture, and visit their own psychologists!

Although you may not want to extend your efforts quite that

far, your customers will appreciate it when you recognize their entourage with a few amenities. For instance, Rollin' Oats health food store in St. Petersburg, Florida, has miniature shopping carts that children can push around as they help mommy shop. Publix supermarket always has free balloons for children, cupcakes on your child's birthday, and antibacterial wipes available for kids with sticky hands. Be sure to ask mom or dad, outside of the child's hearing, before offering treats.

Have you considered having printed materials available with a larger font for those who can't see very well? Or benches available for those who need to rest?

A teller in the drive-through at a Florida branch of Wachovia Bank always has treats for the dogs that are in the cars with their owners. My Maltese, Snowball, gets excited waiting for the "magic tube" to come down the chute because she knows there's a treat just for her. I wouldn't dare change banks!

Think about all of the people who travel with your usual customer. How could you give them a little bit of the star treatment?

Take Five: Train Your Team Well

A few months ago, I was in an airport riding on a shuttle from one concourse to another. The shuttle car was full of people, and behind me was a party of three—two airport employees and one woman who was in a wheelchair. One of the employees was apparently escorting the woman in the wheelchair to her gate and, like me, they were taking the shuttle to get there. While they rode, the two employees carried on a loud conversation with each other about another employee and how she had refused to "do wheelchairs." "I'm sick and tired of doing wheelchairs," one of them said. "Why should I have to do all the wheelchairs when she gets out of it?" "I know," the other one exclaimed. "I've pushed three wheelchairs already today, and I'm just going to refuse from now on."

Wow. I didn't know what to do, quite frankly. I couldn't believe they were having this conversation right in front of this woman, without regard to her feelings at all. I looked at the woman in the wheelchair and smiled at her. She smiled back and lifted her shoulders in resignation. I refrained from commenting, thinking the woman had already been embarrassed enough. But I wonder if I made a mistake. Someone should have called those young women on their behavior.

My personal opinion was that this incident would have been best avoided by better hiring practices. However, it did bring to mind the realization that during the course of any given day in a service situation, you and your team will welcome people of many different circumstances into your place of business. While you may have a written policy of not discriminating on the basis of age, race, gender, religion, sexual orientation, or disabilities, you may need to consider educating your team members on exactly what this policy entails.

Are your team members armed with information about the special needs of older customers, and patient enough to give them the same level of customer service everyone else receives even though they may move a little more slowly? Are they familiar with the correct language to use when referring to a person with a disability? For instance, the young women above kept referring to pushing wheelchairs when they were actually escorting a person who was using a wheelchair. Even worse, they talked about that woman as if she weren't even there. Are there members of your team who assume that any teenager in the building means trouble, or are they as welcoming with young people as they are with people their own age? Are your team members willing and able to greet every single person, regardless of ethnicity, gender, presumed sexual orientation, or religion, with the respect we all deserve, even if their personal opinions differ from that of the person in front of them?

Hiring people who are kind, respectful, and caring, and honestly love people is one way to ensure that all your customers will be treated like stars. However, even the most well-meaning people don't always know how to behave when confronted with situations that are new to them. Continual training is the way to be sure that your team members have the information they need to accommodate when necessary, and give every human being you do business with The Celebrity Experience.

There is an old saying in the theater that goes like this: There are no small roles, only small actors. This means that regardless of the size of your part in the play, or the amount of time you spend on stage, you are an integral part of the performance. If the actors in the bit parts treat their roles as unimportant or are treated that way by the rest of the cast, the show will suffer as a result.

While you may have different kinds of experiences for people who can pay more for them, the general experience of being treated well and receiving good customer service should not be reserved for just a few. Those who give excellent customer service to just a few select customers do not really give good customer service at all.

When the next person who walks through your door or calls you on the phone prompts you to ask yourself, "Are they anybody?" remember to answer "yes," and go about giving that person the star treatment.

The Celebrity Next Door

WHILE DOING RESEARCH for this book, I had the great pleasure of meeting Gene Perret. Gene is the author of 20 books on comedy and an Emmy Award winning writer who has written for shows such as *Mama's Family*, *Welcome Back, Kotter*, and the *Carol Burnett Show*. He also wrote comedy for Bob Hope longer than any other of his many writers. You may have read his book, *Talk About Hope*.

Which is exactly what Gene and I did. We talked about Hope. He said to me, "Bob Hope was the best boss I ever had."

When I asked what he meant, he told me four things:

He was understanding. "Like anyone else, comedy writers have their good days and their bad days. I mean, every painting Picasso did didn't hang in the Louvre. Some comedians expected their writers to be *on* 24/7. If you had an off day once in a while, Bob would say 'Ah, the other guys will be on.'"

He was appreciative. "In those days, most comedians didn't want the general public to know that anyone other than themselves wrote their material. Bob, on the other hand, would bring his writers on stage to receive applause with him whenever he had the chance. He would also call you personally if he liked what you wrote."

He knew his business. "As his writer, I could feel confident in what I was doing because I knew without a doubt that he knew what he was doing."

And then Gene said to me:

"He was the celebrity, but when I was in his presence he made me feel important. When Bob was dealing with you, you were the most important person in the room. Why one time I remember he even made the secretary of defense wait on hold because he was talking to me!"

Let's think about that for a moment.

When I was in his presence, he made me feel important.

Isn't that what we've been talking about all along? Making others feel important and special? Treating others as if they were the celebrities?

Which brings us to the celebrities who work for you—your employees. If you want them to make your customers feel good, then they have to feel good about themselves. Often, when I ask people what is done to show appreciation for employees where they work, I receive answers such as, "We have an employee appreciation breakfast once a month," or "We get pins when we've been there for five years." Great, for a start. But make no mistake. These are events. They are tools. They aren't employee appreciation.

Employee appreciation is *more* than a special event!

Don't get me wrong. Employee breakfasts and pins are great. However, it's your day-to-day habit of acknowledging, recognizing, rewarding, respecting, and caring about your employees that really makes the difference. If you don't have that as a foundation, the parties, the pins, the pizza, and the plaques won't make a bit of difference. In order to be meaningful, all of those tokens must be backed up by a complete culture of caring.

Ask yourself this question. When employees or coworkers are in my presence, how do I make each one feel like the most important person in the room?

Let me tell you about a group of people who have perfected the art of rolling out the red carpet for their employees and making their coworkers feel and shine like stars!

Go Jobing!

When I first met Mariah Bieber, the community relations manager for the Orange County, California, division of Jobing.com, I was struck by her vivaciousness and unbridled enthusiasm. She approached me after I had given a speech about employee recognition and morale for a group of human resources directors. Mariah told me, "Our company does everything you just talked about! We strive to be different from other companies and really work to roll out the red carpet for both our coworkers and our customers. We've just got to get together!"

Her excitement was infectious, and Mariah and I stayed in touch. As I learned more about Jobing.com, I could see why she was hooked. The people at Jobing.com, a company that connects employers with job seekers in their local market through the Internet, know how to do it right. Their profits have doubled yearly since its inception, and they've been on *Inc.* magazine's list of Fastest Growing Companies. Twice. They've also been named on several local Best Places to Work lists. You're about to find out why.

"When you have engaged employees, you increase the likelihood of having engaged clients," says Nicole Spracale, VP of Talent Development. "We set that standard for our employees the very first time we meet them."

When candidates arrive for their interviews at Jobing.com, they are seated in a very homey reception area. Between the time they arrive and the actual interview, "we make it a point to kill them with kindness," says Nicole. It is not unusual for a candidate to remark, "Goodness, I think 70 people welcomed me and offered me something to drink!" The candidates are definitely not ignored. During the interview, recruiters look between the lines for qualities like passion and energy. They want to know about the key motivators of those applying for a position. Candidates who are a good fit will leave exclaiming, "This is it! I know Jobing.com is the place for me."

Once they offer a position to an applicant, the HR team immediately sends a welcome letter, but the welcome does not stop there. Prior to the new recruit's first day of training, regular communication takes place. Says Nicole, "I, or one of the recruiters, will touch base at least two times per week until they start, with bits of information and to let them know how glad we are to have them on board." The team members of the new recruit also send welcoming e-mails, which helps newcomers to make connections prior to their first day at work. Teams will host a special lunch to welcome new coworkers. General managers will also call with their personal welcome to let the newcomers know what to expect, answer any questions, and provide them with any contact numbers they might need.

There is a method to the madness. "We're trying to model what we expect of them," Nicole tells me. "For instance, if we've hired a recruitment specialist, we might send a book on how to wow people in the recruitment process, just as they are experiencing now."

All recent hires are flown into Arizona for a two-week orientation at the home office. They arrive on a Sunday and are put up in a nearby hotel, where they will find a gift basket in their room. "Lunch and dinner are catered in, and we will often take them to a local event. We treat them like honored guests because we want them to treat our customers the same way."

Meanwhile, family members at home have received a gift card along with a note thanking them for "allowing us to borrow your loved one for two weeks' time."

During the orientation, the recruits get to meet with the entire leadership team who communicate how committed they are to the success of the newcomers and everyone who works at Jobing.com.

Knowing that little things mean a lot, the Jobing.com team will even print out their new recruits' boarding passes before it's time to fly home.

Once the new recruits have their first on-the-job success, their peers will send cheers via e-mail. Life at Jobing.com has begun.

Once an employee starts, what is life like in their new office?

One thing you will notice that is unique to the Jobing.com culture is that we hug. We hug a lot. This, we know, is unusual for a workplace. We also understand that hugging is not everyone's bag, and that's okay. They will definitely notice employees hugging while they are here interviewing. We just encourage new recruits to find their own comfort level with this, and it will be respected. But, there is definitely hugging at Jobing.com.

Having fun at work is also part of the corporate culture at Jobing.com. While other companies plan a theme day once in a while, having fun is expected in their offices. Employees get free soda, free coffee, free Jobing.com clothing.

Once employees start, their general manager receives a list of their favorites: their favorite restaurant, favorite store, and so on. This enables managers to get to know their new team members as human beings and personalize future recognition efforts.

In its commitment to being extraordinary in all it does, Jobing.com offers benefits such as a monthly vehicle stipend after one year of employment, a 60-day sabbatical after seven years, and free access to a collection of more than 600 business books, videos, and CDs. Excellent education is one of the company values, and employees get 50 hours of training per year, in addition to 100 hours of leadership training. The company will pay for associate, bachelor's, and master's degrees and has its own corporate MBA program.

"Again," reminds Nicole, "we expect a lot out of them in exchange for all of this." Compensation is tied to performance. They are also evaluated on items such as being a leader, living the company values, and teamwork. Management makes no apologies for expecting the best of those who work for the company, and employees give the best in return.

Every quarter Jobing.com has what it calls its "road show." The executive team hits all regional markets and flies out every employee who is too far away to drive to the event. There, CEO Aaron Matos addresses every single question and concern that was brought up on the employee satisfaction survey. The surveys, made up of open-ended questions, ask employees to share suggestions for product changes and enhancements, offer examples of changes that would help them do their jobs better, and finish the sentence "If I were CEO, I would. . . ."

As Matos addresses each response, he does not edit anything out, unless it would embarrass a staffer. However, those on the leadership team who are named in the survey must be ready to hear about it at that meeting. This is the Leadership Team Report Card.

How's all this working for them? Check out the company's web site and you'll see the photos of the entire team next to testimonials about Jobing.com. You'll see words like passion, success, excitement, and enthusiasm. You'll see phrases like "the greatest company I have ever worked for." But it's the numbers that will impress you the most.

Jobing.com's employee satisfaction scores ranged from 4.5 to 4.8 or 4.9 out of a possible score of 5.0. They get better every year. As you can probably predict, Jobing.com's clients are also very happy.

As I learned more about this company, I was reminded of an experience I once had after I gave a presentation on red carpet employee appreciation. One audience member remarked to me that "there is not a single workplace on earth that is as wonderful as the one you just described." Although I tend to have a more positive outlook than she apparently did, I began to worry that perhaps she was right. Perhaps I had invented this imaginary workplace that, in reality, didn't exist. Then I met the people at Jobing.com.

"We're certainly not perfect," warns Nicole. Of course not. What company is? But they do know how to get the best from their employees and give them the star treatment.

Here are some action tips to help you do the same:

Take One: Roll Out the Red Carpet

Take Two: Share Cheers and Chuckles

Take Three: Give Excellent Training

Take Four: Provide Incredible Benefits

Take Five: Practice Accountability

Take One: Roll Out the Red Carpet

The people at Jobing.com know how important it is to roll the red carpet out prior to every new employee's first day on the job. They know the welcome needs to start from the moment candidates walk in for the interview, and especially after they have said the magic words—"You're hired!" Remember your first few days at your current job? Were you excited? Nervous? Did you worry about your ability to accomplish the tasks given to you or the impression you would make on your new coworkers? Perhaps you were concerned about the impression your new coworkers would make on you.

You would not be alone if you were feeling a little lost during your probationary period. Many people do. By realizing this, and going out of your way to help make new employees feel comfortable, you are giving them the best chance for success, which of course contributes to your own success.

If you want to do a better job at giving a hero's welcome to your new recruits, here's the best thing you can do. Ask. Maria Motsavage of Ideal Senior Living uses this tip to get feedback from her customers. Here I've adapted it to get employee feedback. Ask your current employees how welcome they felt, on a scale of 1 to 10, with 10 being the best, when they started their job at your company. If their answers are anything less than 10s, ask, "What could we have done to make it a 10?" Let them tell you how it's done.

To get you started, here are some ideas from people at Jobing.com and others that you might consider.

The Preview: Before Their First Day

- Send a welcome letter to your new recruits letting them know how glad you are to have them join your work family. Include an invitation to lunch with the boss.

- Keep the connections strong by touching base several times between the date of hire and the first day on the job. Give your new team members as much information as they need at this point and answer any of their questions. Send goodies, and, if you can, "Give 'Em Their Chicken Soup." A great idea is sending a book that mirrors the kind of service you want them to give your customers, as Jobing.com does. Shameless plug alert: How about *The Celebrity Experience?*
- Involve your current employees in welcoming their new coworkers. Remember that sometimes it's tough for new people to break into the already close-knit group that is your team. Put the responsibility on existing employees to be proactive in involving their new coworkers. They can send e-mails, cards, or even do it the old-fashioned way and pick up the telephone. When newcomers are reached out to in this way, they feel as if they have connections at work before they even start.

The Premiere: Their First Day

- Be present and available. Don't schedule your new team members to come in when you and their supervisors have meetings or other pressing matters to attend to. Once, after hearing me share this in a speech, an HR director came up to me and said, "You know, you really got me thinking. Up until this point, we've always had our new employees start their first day by coming in at the same time as everyone else. They arrive 15 to 20 minutes early, all dressed up, and wait in the lobby alone. Then three to five minutes after start time, the current employees rush right past them, grabbing their coffee and chatting with their coworkers. From now on I'm going to have new employees start 30 minutes later, and talk to our current employees about giving them a warmer reception."

While I'm sure it's a slight exaggeration that 70 people greet the interviewees at Jobing.com, saying hello and offering them drinks, it certainly is a team effort to make everyone feel at home. Again, enlist the entire team in the red carpet welcome by asking them to be proactive about reaching out to newcomers.

- Remember the "Red Carpet Arrivals" chapter? Why not enlist some of those techniques in this situation as well. Reserve a parking space with a sign that has the new employee's name on it, put up a welcome banner, have a greeter waiting in the lobby or at the door on the first day. Roll out a red carpet! Decorate the office or workspace. Put pictures of new employees up on the bulletin board and invite coworkers to post welcome messages around the photos.

- Have a welcome lunch where everyone can get to know the new people.

- Ask your new team members to fill out a favorites list. This will give a boss information to use when purchasing meaningful rewards. A gift card to a favorite restaurant has much more impact than one from the stack you keep in your desk drawer.

- Appoint Celebrity Ambassadors to take new coworkers under their wings. One word of caution, though. Make sure to select people who love their jobs and are going to be positive about the company. You definitely don't want an ambassador who is filling the new recruits' ears with gossip and complaints. (If you've got a person on your team like that, you may want to consider whether the job is a good fit, but that's a subject for another book.)

- Have your new employees' work area completely cleaned and prepared. One CEO told me when she was hired, she found all manner of things in her office, including the dirty socks of the previous CEO! Is the work space clean and neat? Do the new employees have all the materials and information they need at their fingertips? Balloons and flowers on the desk or at their locker would be a nice touch.

- As they do at Jobing.com, treat your employees as you want them to treat your customers.

Rehearsal: Their Orientation

- Take a look at your orientation process. Are you guilty of shoving boring movies in the DVD player and calling that training? I personally have walked into such a so-called training session only to find new employees snoring away. (In which case, you might also want to look at your hiring process, but again, that's another book.) The people at Jobing.com spend two weeks in orientation before they ever start their jobs. Every single leader on the management team is there to greet them and cheer them on. The first half day of the orientation is spent just on the values of the company and how crucial living those values at work is to their success. How does your orientation measure up? Are you giving your new employees the impression that you expect the best of them by giving them the best of you at the very start?

- Have fun! Even some orientation presentations done by live human beings can be real snoozers if they're not spiced up a bit. Play games, give prizes, use music, tell stories, get them laughing! People learn best when they are laughing! Here's a great tip given to me by Gail Hahn, MA, CSP, CLL, CEO (Chief Energizing Officer) of FUN*cilitators, a division of Energize Enterprises, LLC:

> One of the fun ways I've facilitated with former teams and one that I advise my clients to use is to have a new employee orientation scavenger hunt. Give them a list of clues and things to pick up from different departments

and new people to meet. Each person may have a stapler or a box of pens or sticky notes for the newcomer. Then team them up with a sponsor to take them around to meet and greet and get the lay of the land. Make it fun— have a party in their honor to welcome them instead of waiting until they leave the company to throw them a party.

- Check in periodically throughout the first few weeks to see how your new employees are faring. Have lunch and encourage coworkers to invite the newcomers to lunch as well.
- Remember to ask your new team members to evaluate the orientation process and give suggestions for improvement. Make the questions open-ended so you will get more helpful feedback. Ask, "What was the best thing about your first 90 days?" and "What was the worst thing about your first 90 days?" You'll get much better answers than if you simply ask them to rate you on a scale.

Of course, you will want to keep that red carpet out much longer than the first 90 days. Which brings us to the next action step.

Take Two: Share Cheers and Chuckles

One of the best perks of being a celebrity is also the simplest one. Applause! It's often what drives a person to pursue a career in acting. There's no doubt about it, celebrities love to receive applause. Guess what? So do your employees. In fact, Gallup polls have consistently shown that the number one reason why people leave their jobs is that they don't feel appreciated. While some people may prefer a private compliment here and there and others revel in more public recognition, all workers want to feel noticed and appreciated for their accomplishments at work. Here are some ways you can ensure they do:

Cheers!

- **Celebrate accomplishments.** The Jobing.com team is right on when they make a big deal out of a new employee's first appointment. It's that kind of support and celebration that keeps us motivated to continue when difficulties arise. Here's another great idea by Kim Kotecki of KimandJason.com:

> My husband Jason is a member of the National Speakers Association (NSA). We love being a part of the NSA family! We have a group of five of us from our local chapter who have formed a mastermind group in which we meet monthly to work together to help each other grow our businesses and ourselves. They are, in many ways, like a department in our company. We have a cool thing that we've started that involves sharing our "woo hoos." Basically, whenever one of us has something fun to share that he or she is excited about or proud of, that person e-mails the group the "woo hoo" and we all send e-mails to celebrate with the excited person. This goes for business and personal achievements. It's been a great way to stay connected and support each other, especially since we only meet monthly.

- **When you see it, say it.** Many times we might think something wonderful about employees or coworkers, but refrain from saying it out loud. We figure, "Heck, they already know how much I admire them." Perhaps so, but we all love to hear positive feedback about ourselves and our work. Get in the habit of verbalizing your specific praise whenever you think it. If you see employees or coworkers behave in a way that you admire, tell them on the spot. Don't wait and decide you'll tell them later. Don't assume they already know. See it, and say it. This is the quickest way to make the most impact in terms of recognition, and it doesn't take a lot of time or even cost a cent.

- **Write them up.** We certainly waste no time writing up employees when they've done something wrong. What if we wrote them up for the things they do right? When employees do something praiseworthy, let them know on the spot, but then also jot a note down and stick it in their file. Then when it's time to do employees' performance evaluations, you have a record of very specific things they did well and can give much more valuable feedback. If you are a coworker, write it up and give it to the supervisor. Cheers from peers are important as well as the ones that come from the boss.

Celebrity Dish

One of my favorite memories is when we were sitting in the audience at the Grammy Awards, as nominees, along with Aretha Franklin, Earth Wind and Fire, and a couple of other top-shelf entertainers. When they called The Commodores name out as winners for *Nightshift*, I rose up out of my seat without the aid of my legs!!! So far, that's the feeling to beat.

J.D., member, The Commodores

- **Celebrate milestones.** Create a culture of celebration by recognizing the important events in the work and personal lives of your team. There are many reasons to celebrate including work anniversaries, birthdays, graduations, and even citizenship days. When one of the supervisors where I once worked became an American citizen, we held a big red, white, and blue shindig complete with hot dogs and apple pie.

To be truly extraordinary, go beyond what any of your team members would expect. Nido Qubein personally calls every single one of his faculty and staff members to wish them a happy birthday. He is the president of the university! When they receive their calls, almost every staff member exclaims that they have never before received such a personalized birthday wish from another university president. Then again, Nido has made a pledge to be extraordinary.

While not all companies are ready for employees who hug each other as much as Jobing.com's employees do, there is room for laughter in every workplace. Remember Victor Borge's quote, "Laughter is the shortest distance between two people." By creating a workplace culture that includes laughter and play as a given, you have a head start in helping people work better as a team and develop friendships at work. And this can only help your morale as well as your customer service levels. A Gallup poll of more than five million individuals revealed that people who have at least one best friend at work are seven times more likely to be engaged, and have more engaged customers.

Chuckles

- **People make their own fun.** Let your team members know right away that you encourage laughter in the workplace. Model it, talk about it, put it in their job descriptions, make it one of your values. Then get out of their way. When people know they are allowed to have fun, they will make their own fun.

- **Healthy fun.** Be sure to define fun in your workplace. Fun does not mean making fun of coworkers, ethnic or religious groups, sexual orientation, or the company itself. It does mean celebrating with each other, cheering each other on, laughing about and learning from mistakes, and taking the work seriously and themselves lightly.
- **Hoopla.** It's amazing what you can turn into a special event. One audience member of a credit union organization told me they have what they call "Friday Night Dancing." Every Friday, when the credit union closes, they turn the music on and employees dance for 15 full minutes. How's the hoopla where you work?

Celebrity Sighting

Diana Gardner is a practice manager who has managed medical offices since 1990. Whenever she feels that morale is too low or gossip is too high, she announces to everyone that they should meet her at the time clock before opening on the next Friday morning. She shows up with doughnut holes, homemade peanut butter fudge, or something of that yummy sort and asks each person coming in to tell her something they caught someone doing right during the previous week. For each right thing, they can have one of the treats she's brought. Says Diana, "It was almost funny how the physicians who complained the loudest could find so many things to compliment so many employees on!" What a great way to remind people to focus on the positive.

Take Three: Give Excellent Training

It goes without saying that if you want your team to give red carpet customer service, you've got to train them to do just that. The training at most of the companies profiled in this book is extensive and ongoing. It is the key to consistent red carpet service.

Some of the celebrity service companies had very creative ways of training their employees. For instance, Scott Graham, CEO of XPACS sends his employees to sell candy with some kids out on the street corner on their first day of work. "I saw how imaginative these kids were with their selling techniques, and that's the kind of imagination I need in my staff. They can see right out of the gate that we're a company that wants out-of-the-box thinking."

Also, many of the companies make a point to go beyond providing training solely focused on the employee's job. If you have a complete culture of caring, it means you care about your employees whether they stay with you or they leave. Companies like Jobing.com provide training to help the employee be better (and then the company is better) versus providing training that's only going to help the company be better (focused solely on the job).

Dan Maddux, whose employees at the American Payroll Association often have to travel and speak in public, offers training on etiquette in restaurants, how to hail a cab, how to dress for success, and presentation skills. Treating your employees like celebrities means making them feel good and prepared for a better future, whether it's working for you or for someone else.

Take Four: Provide Incredible Benefits

If you really want to treat your employees like stars, take a look at your benefits package. The founders of Jobing.com decided right from the start that they wanted to be extraordinary in every way. This is why, in addition to the typical benefits companies give to employees, Jobing.com offers items like a monthly vehicle stipend, 60-day sabbaticals, and free education that I mentioned earlier.

Companies that serve celebrities, such as Marquis Jet, also go all out for their staff members. Says Jesse Itzler, "We have an incredible retention rate internally, and people generally like to work here. We've created a great culture, and we spend a lot of time and money making sure that people who work here have a good experience and get along with each other, and everyone is rolling along. We have all the typical benefits that other companies have, but then we have what we like to call 'Marquis Style' benefits." Marquis Style benefits include an estate outside of New York City, called the Marquis Estate, which has a full staff that includes a personal chef and a masseuse. Employees can sign up to take their families there for a weekend or so, enjoy the swimming pool, tennis courts, and time away from the city. They share front row seats at Yankees games, and receive manicures and pedicures once a week. Motivational speakers, such as *New York Times* best-selling author Jake Steinfeld, come in about once a month. There is also a chef on staff who comes in about twice a week to make lunch for everyone.

Of course, they expect the best from their employees, which is why they give the best to their employees.

Take Five: Practice Accountability

Whether it's a company that serves Hollywood and sports celebrities or a company that gives red carpet customer service to everyday people, all of them had this in common. They expect a great deal from their employees.

As Rita Tateel of The Celebrity Source says, "Errors are just not acceptable in my business. If, for example, you misspell a celebrity's name, your letter will just go in the trash." The difference between celebrities and the rest of us is that celebrities will head elsewhere if they don't receive the best service. We, on the other hand, have gotten used to a world where good customer service is a buzz word and not an actuality. We complain about substandard service, but we accept it as a fact of life and continue to do business as usual.

However, the companies that have made it to our Celebrity Experience Hall of Fame have decided that business as usual is not for them. They treat their employees very well, but they lay it on the line in terms of what is expected of them, and they give them all the tools they need to succeed. John Wood of Hub Plumbing told me, "We are like a cult culture. We run our company a certain way, and you are either all the way in, or you are out before your 30 days are up." It's not that the owners of these companies are trying to be harsh. It is simply that they know that your service is only as good as your most disengaged employee. Giving extraordinary service is not for everyone. However, if you decide you are committed to giving your customers The Celebrity Experience, then you need to be sure everyone on the team is as committed as you are.

The good news is, the ones who get it, love it! They are energized by the very thought of being extraordinary. "It's about more than money," says John. "It's about being a team that feeds each other. I wish you could see my guys at 6:30 A.M. on Monday mornings. They are wide awake, sitting in a circle, firing ideas one right after another. It's incredible!"

Celebrity Sighting

When Selina Man, owner of Café Chocolate of Lititz, Pennsylvania, brings on a new team member she tells them she expects three things of them:

1. *They must love people. "No exceptions—even cranky people."*
2. *They must love food. "If they don't they won't appreciate the lengths we go to to ensure the organic food in the cafe is the right quality. We are very strict about this."*

3. *They must love to learn. "People who don't love to learn can get defensive. Those who do love to learn, flourish."*

In return, she promises her team three things:

1. *We will have fun every day.*
2. *We will keep learning every day.*
3. *We will make money every day.*

Selina also practices open book accounting with her entire team. "Every single team member knows the daily details of the financials of the cafe. How can I get people to take ownership of their work in the cafe if they don't know their impact? It's noble to help people far away, but if that does not extend to the people right there working with you, then it isn't real!"

When you choose to work with people who have star potential, treat them like stars and expect them to shine like stars, they will in turn, treat your customers like stars. Still not convinced? Here's one more example that proves when you put your employees first, they will put your customers first.

Arthur Keith, the general manager of the Gaylord Opryland Resort and Convention Center, told me this:

This is a great hotel. Like any company, though, we've gone through some changes. We opened our Delta atrium in 1997, and it really took us four to five years to get the right staff in place and really run this now-expansive complex correctly. In the middle of that change, Colin Reed came on board as the new CEO of Gaylord Entertainment. Previously, Colin was the CFO of Harris Entertainment in Las Vegas, so he's a financier and a hotelier. But what's amazing is that he also gets the people side.

When he joined the company, the first thing he said was "It's all about the people." We had put our product first, service secondary, and our STARS (employees) somewhere after that. Colin said, "Our STARS didn't fail Opryland. Opryland failed our STARS. We need to make sure we take care of our people."

That's when they rolled out their quarterly bonus plan (discussed in "The Chicago Pizza Principle.") In 2005, we paid out close to $900,000 in bonuses to our STARS. Now we spend a lot of energy and resources around what we call our STARS First Culture. Our end result is the same one that our competitors want and that is to have a great guest experience. We just don't believe we get there by focusing on the guest first. We get there by focusing on the STARS first.

Here's what that looks like at the Gaylord:

There is an entire group of people in their HR department that is just focused on solid communication with the STARS that is high-energy and fun. Every quarter we have all-star rallies (employee meetings) and we bring everyone together for these massive productions. We even have our own in-house all-star bands (a la *The Tonight Show*) that accompany the updates. Since we're a music town we've got a lot of musicians who work for us. So for each meeting, 12 different people get together and form the band. There are drums, horns, harmonicas, singers, and backup singers. The band is there just to create energy for the meeting, while we update every employee about what's happening with the company, customer satisfaction scores, and employee satisfaction scores.

In 2007, the theme at the Gaylord is "Passion." So for one rally all the leaders, including General Manager Arthur Keith, wore bright red tuxedos for the event. "Red top hats. Red shoes. Red ruffled shirt. It was crazy."

Training is key, and so is communication. Arthur will have town hall meetings when he goes to every department, sits in a room with the STARS and ask them these questions.

1. What do we stop?
2. What do we start?
3. What do we continue?

STARS answer these questions on Post-It notes, without their leaders in the room. Then Arthur goes through the notes and starts the conversations.

When Colin Reed, CEO of Gaylord Entertainment, visits the Gaylord properties he will ask the STARS their opinions of what's going on and how leadership treats them. However, here's the piece that impressed me to no end. Every single month he opens his phone lines on a specific day for "Call the CEO." Any person who works within the entire company can pick up the phone and give him a call. They can call to complain, share ideas, give praise, or simply say hello.

What are the results of this STARS First Culture? Well, I've already shared how their customer satisfaction scores are going up and up. However, Arthur Keith really brought it home when he told me this:

We've got so many more growth opportunities now since starting the STARS First Culture. Our profit goals have gone from $50 million to $100 million, because we are now positioned to the point where we are confident we can accomplish it. Our parent company [Gaylord Entertainment] has invested $400 million dollars in our business. From a business perspective, you don't make an investment like that in a company that you think is shaky or doesn't have a good strong culture. Each of our wins has started by putting our STARS first.

If you want your employees to roll out the red carpet for your customers, model that expectation by giving them a little star treatment. As you can see from the examples above, your company has much to gain by putting your people first.

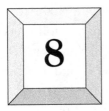

Branding Ovations

MOVIE STARS IN HOLLYWOOD and sports celebrities are more than actors and athletes—they are brands. In the minds of the audience, each celebrity stands for a specific something, which is cultivated by a carefully crafted media and marketing campaign.

Jo-Ann Geffen, owner of JAG Entertainment, a public relations and celebrity placement firm, has helped many superstars define their brands. "We start by finding out the expectations of the celebrity. What are their goals? What image do they hold of themselves? How do they perceive their areas of expertise and who does that appeal to? Once we have a clear idea of who the performer is and how they want to be perceived, we then decide which markets we want to target. It has to make sense. We wouldn't, for instance, want to promote a rap artist in *Ladies Home Journal.*"

Once a brand is created, though, it's up to the artist to deliver the goods. "The unfortunate thing is that with all the media out there, people are becoming stars overnight. Will their star continue to shine? That remains to be seen."

Much of it depends on the artists being very clear as to who they are and then being consistent with that image in the eyes of the public. For instance, Paris Hilton is a party girl. She knows she's a party girl, and she perpetuates that image with everything she says and does. Her fans and followers expect her to be a party girl. On the other hand, if Kate Winslet, who is known as a serious actress, a loving wife and mother, and a down-to-earth woman with whom other women relate, were to suddenly be photographed hanging out with a variety of men and giving less-than-stellar performances on the silver screen, her brand would take some serious hits. She would no longer be credible. She wouldn't be the Kate Winslet her fans perceive her to be. As a result, her marketability would falter. Fortunately, Kate Winslet is a living and breathing example of her brand.

As a case in point, take a look at the Martha Stewart brand. Martha Stewart was an incredibly successful author, television celebrity, and the CEO of her own company, Martha Stewart Living Omnimedia (MSLO). She was known to her fans as the model of perfection. Her cooking, crafting, gardening, and home decorating—all perfect. She was meticulous and detailed, and gave everything just the right touch. And it was "a good thing." She was the picture of success, and in 2001, Martha Stewart Living Omnimedia was worth $295.6 million.

Then, in 2002, something happened that was completely contradictory to Martha's brand as the perfect homemaker. She was accused of insider trading. From that point forward, her entire image changed. She was portrayed in the media as an unethical, greedy, corporate monster. She ultimately was convicted of the crime and went to prison for a five-month term. When she was released, she was sentenced to house arrest for another few months. As a result, Martha stepped down as CEO of MSLO, resigned as a board member of the New York Stock Exchange, and was barred from serving as a director of a public company. (Hence, she couldn't return to the director's position of her own company.)

In 2004, the net worth of MSLO was down more than $100 million to $187.4 million. Martha Stewart's personal holdings went from $1 billion to $500 million in just a few short years. She is currently doing what she can to rebuild her brand, and it may be working. However, there is no question as to the importance of living up to your brand in word and deed in the world of celebrity.

The same is true in the world of noncelebrity business. You can develop a slick marketing campaign that includes a catchy slogan, the perfect colors, and a fabulous web site, but if you and everyone involved with your company do not deliver the goods, you might as well throw the marketing materials in the wastebasket.

I found a fantastic company located in Boston, Massachusetts, that has it all. They've got the look, the colors, the marketing materials, even red carpets, and they deliver the goods.

Plumbers . . . On the Red Carpet

If you live in Boston, Massachusetts, chances are you are aware of Hub Plumbing & Mechanical Company, Inc. Seven days a week, you can spot one or more of its five custom-designed service trucks on the road. You just can't miss them. They are large, and bright red with the company name and logo on the side, in gold. If you've been to the Dorchester Day Parade, or any number of community events, you've probably seen Hub Plumbing trucks and its plumbers proudly wearing their bright red shirts with the Hub logo. And if you've ever had a leaky faucet, a clogged drain, or a broken garbage disposal, you might have watched in amazement as the well-groomed plumber, wearing an ID badge and shoe covers, *literally* rolled out a red carpet and carefully placed his tools on them to avoid destroying your floor.

John Wood, CEO of Hub Plumbing & Mechanical, has given a lot of thought and time to creating an image for his company that is miles away from what you'd expect. Plumbers who work for Hub are to wear no jewelry and have well trimmed or no facial hair. They wear crisp red shirts that have the Hub logo embroidered in gold. ID badges are mandatory. Their well-fitting pants are pressed and held up with a belt. (No "plumber-butt" at Hub!) And they will hand you a glossy red business card and wait to be invited into your home. "Many people are nervous being alone in their home with a plumber. I've purposefully made my guys look like dorks," John laughs. "I want them to look nonthreatening."

Yes, John Wood wants you to remember Hub Plumbing. Everyone in the company, including apprentices, has business cards. They give out slick folders, fun magnets, and dry erase boards with the Hub logo on it. They leave behind Hub Tags to help you identify valve shutoffs, and they label your appliances with the install date, the next necessary service date, and the name of your technician. They've even been known to replace your toilet paper with a new roll bearing the Hub logo!

But John Wood knows something else, too. He knows that branding is not about the trucks, the carpets, or the toilet paper. It's about the service. If John and his team weren't consistent in the service they provide, the red trucks, the red uniforms, and the red carpets would simply be decoration. And if Hub Plumbing & Mechanical just relied on decor and didn't deliver the goods, it would not have grown from a one-man operation to a $1.5-million business with 11 employees in just six short years.

When you call Hub Plumbing, any time of the day or night, a live person answers the phone. These frontline representatives have undergone extensive training, so they can answer all of your questions effectively. In fact, the conversation is so thorough that they answer questions you didn't even know you had.

They get all the information they need in order to help you, plus a backup phone number and e-mail address . . . just in case.

Next, you receive an e-mail from your plumber. He tells you approximately when to expect him, what his specialties are, and all about his family and his hobbies. As John says, "When people hire a plumber, their expectations are low. Our guys have personality!"

Did I mention that the e-mail is in HTML format and a photo of your plumber is included? In fact, visit www.hubplumbing.com and you will see the photos of every plumber and apprentice plumber who works for Hub, along with a short biographical description. When I went on a ride-around with Joe Wood (John's brother, who works as a technician for the company), one customer told me, "It was the web site that attracted me first. The colors really stood out to me. And they were the only company that put the names and photos of their technicians on the web site. To me, that's like signing off on your work. It told me that Hub was building a customer-centric company, and I haven't used anyone else since."

The day of the visit, your plumber calls when he's on his way to the job. If he is running late, he will call in plenty of time to see if you want to wait or if you would rather reschedule. Assuming the best, you would soon look out your window and see the bright red Hub Plumbing truck roll up to the house. The Hub plumber will park in front of your house—never in the driveway. He wouldn't want to destroy your beautiful flower garden when backing up.

Once you have invited your plumber in, he puts plastic covers over his shoes to keep from marking up your carpet. And he lays down the red carpet with the Hub logo, and places his tools like surgical instruments on it. It's their Red Carpet Service.

So far, does this sound like any plumber you know?

Joe Wood tells me, "Plumbers have a certain reputation for not showing up on time, looking unkempt, and overcharging.

Most people don't know there is any other way. The guys I've met who work for other companies just think that's the way to do business. But I knew my brother was building his company differently. I knew there was a way to look sharp and pay attention to customer service."

When the job is complete to your satisfaction, you will sign off on it and receive a red foil invoice. You might notice that the Hub plumber has left the work space better than he found it—a Hub policy.

You will receive a thank-you note from your plumber and a five-question survey to make sure everything was done right. John Wood calls them "happy calls." More often than not, the general reaction is overwhelmingly good. "We have 60-percent repeat business." Hub charges by the project, and John will admit he's not the cheapest plumber in Boston. However, "If our customers leave to get a better deal, they always come back saying, 'Darn it, I can't get anyone else to do what you do.'"

John's brand of Red Carpet Service and commitment to "Setting the Standard in the Service Industry" (which is the slogan you'll read on the side of their red trucks) is what keeps the job exciting for his employees. "Donna, I wish you could see my guys at 6:30 A.M. on Monday morning," he tells me. "Most people would be sitting there with their eyes half open. Not my team. They're downing coffee and doughnuts, firing ideas one to another. We get excited when we talk to each other. We're constantly looking for ways to take the service to the next level.

"The thing is, customers don't even know they want this level of service. After they get it, they'll never go back."

True, the red trucks, the red uniforms, and the red carpets make Hub Plumbing & Mechanical stand out in the crowd. But what has truly branded Hub and enabled it to grow is the consistency of the excellent service it offers.

Perhaps you're thinking, "Sounds expensive, Donna."

John's operating costs are about three times those of less professional companies, but his return on investment is 30 percent of the gross, businesswide. Also, his initial investment costs are close to being paid off only six years into the business, so his profit margins will increase from here on in. Even though John reinvested much of his revenue back into the business, he's always been able to turn a profit.

Says John, "Oftentimes entrepreneurs make the mistake of assuming that cost is the only factor for the customer. Quite the contrary. If that were true society would not buy Mercedes, buy their food at Whole Foods, or buy $350.00 Hermes scarves. It's truly all about the service, and I wouldn't run my company any other way."

I witnessed the reaction to this service firsthand when I tagged along with technician Joe Wood. One customer named Diane told me, "I remembered them because I saw their trucks in a local parade. To be honest, I called another company first. I left a message and they never called me back. When I called Hub Plumbing, I got a live person on the phone. They called to tell me the plumber was on his way, and then the plumber called to let me know he was in front of the house. This is not the service I typically receive! I will definitely call them back."

As you read this book, I hope you're getting excited about the possibilities for your company. I hope that you are ready to run out and purchase red carpets to welcome your customers, movie star costumes for your launch party, and new business cards that say, "We give our customers a Celebrity Experience." Marketing materials and set dressing can be fun, help you to stand out in the crowd, and may be worth spending your money on. Yet, make no mistake. It is not the red carpets, but the way you consistently deliver red carpet customer service, that is . . . shall we say . . . priceless! Your brand is not defined by your logo. It is a clear and consistent message that is defined by every action you take and what those actions lead your customers to think and say about you. Your brand is defined by each and every customer experience.

How do celebrities and red carpet customer service companies like Hub Plumbing & Mechanical go about branding their uniqueness? It starts with action!

> **Take One:** Know Who You Are and Who You Want to Be
>
> **Take Two:** Give Your Customers a Consistent Experience
>
> **Take Three:** Own Your Brand
>
> **Take Four:** Creatively Package and Promote Your Brand
>
> **Take Five:** Encourage Personal Branding

Take One: Know Who You Want to Be

If there is one thing that all the Celebrity Experience Hall of Fame companies have in common, it's that their leaders know *exactly* what the company represents and where the future of the company lies. They have a clearly defined sense of who they are, and they are committed to demonstrating their mission and values in every single aspect of their business.

Stop reading right now. Walk up to, or call, one or two of your employees and ask them to recite your company mission statement from memory. Then ask them to tell you what the company values are. When you are done, come back. I'll be waiting.

What did you find out? If your employees are like those in most organizations, they have no idea what the company stands for, and sometimes they aren't even clear as to what is expected of them personally.

Here's the difference between most companies and those who consistently give their customers The Celebrity Experience. While most companies have a mission and values statement, the latter group of companies *actually uses* them as their guiding principles in everything they do. Leaders in these companies ask the questions, "What are we about? What kind of service do we want to deliver? What does that look like in each aspect of our company? What kind of experience do we want a customer to have from the moment he walks through our doors (or visits our web site, or dials our phone number)?" Then they sum up their answers in a way that is clear and understandable to everyone in their company.

The mission of the Celebrity Services Department at Gaylord? To give flawless service. Disney's mission? To make people happy. Mary Kay Cosmetics? To give unlimited opportunity to women. And Hub Plumbing? To set the standard in the service industry by utilizing a professional, friendly, and customer-centric approach. When it comes to values (or service basics, as they are called at Gaylord), all the Celebrity Experience Hall of Fame companies do this—they talk about them. Every chance they get. At every company meeting. With every manager and with every employee. Some, as Tabitha Health Care did, have them printed on wallet-size cards that can be carried around and referred to often. The values of the company become imprinted on the hearts and minds of everyone who works there.

It's not just talk. The Celebrity Experience Hall of Fame companies know what they are and make no compromises when it comes to delivering on their promise to themselves about what they want to be. Wherever they are when they make the commitment to red carpet service is where they start.

For instance, when John Wood of Hub Plumbing noticed

the skittish reaction of a customer when he, a big burly guy, showed up at her front door wearing jeans and a Red Sox T-shirt, he decided to change the perception the public had about plumbers. At that time he was just a one-man business. He cleaned up his vehicle, bought himself some nice pants and a uniform-style shirt, and made himself an ID badge with an index card and a passport photo. "It went over like a trip when I first started it!"

While John was an entrepreneur without a lot of money, he was setting a standard from the starting gate that would help him grow his company into a million-dollar business. From the very beginning, John knew who he was and who he wanted to be, and began branding himself and his company as a leader in red carpet customer service, long before he ever bought the actual red carpets used in his company today.

Decide what you want to be as a company, and then start being that. Right now. No compromises. Begin by taking a realistic look at what you are now. Use customer and employee surveys, customer comments, observation, and bottom-line dollar amounts. Then create a strong, compelling vision of what you want to be. Make it clear and concise—something everyone within your company will understand and remember. Involve the people who will carry out the vision in developing the vision. Define a specific set of behaviors for demonstrating your vision and values. Spend time and money on training so everyone in your company understands your company values and the expected accompanying actions.

Then behave in that manner, and hold everyone in your company accountable for behaving in that manner, as well.

Take Two: Give Your Customers a Consistent Experience

In order for you to have a strong service brand, the service you deliver must be consistent. This means that every single time customers have interactions with your organization, they must experience the same level of service . . . regardless of who in your company they encounter. This means that everyone who represents you in any way must buy in to the specific values and behaviors that you want your company to be known for. If one person in your company delivers service that is inconsistent with your brand, then the perception your customers held in the past will be replaced by a new, negative perception.

To accomplish consistent service, you've got to develop systems and have your employees well trained in how to utilize those systems. What needs to be done, in what order, each and every time, by each and every person who greets a customer on the phone or when they walk through the door? Ride along with one of the Hub plumbers as I did, and you'll notice that they follow the same procedure with every customer. I noticed him wait for each customer to invite him in, and I saw him put his shoe covers on before he entered every house. I watched as Joe thoroughly and systematically explained each estimate. I heard him clarify to everyone that the cost is based on projects not hours. At Hub Plumbing they have systems for everything.

Begin by taking a look at your customer's experience, such as it is now, from the beginning to the end of each interaction. Take away any step in the process that does not add something positive to the customer's experience. Danny Jones, director of operational excellence and innovation for the Gaylord Opryland Resort and Convention Center, takes a look at all customer touch points and tries to eliminate deficiencies. Then he goes to the people who make all the difference—the employees who actually perform the tasks—and questions them about the processes. "I may spend four days in a conference room just talking with the bellmen. We look at every point in their process to see if it actually adds to the customer experience. If it doesn't, it's gone. We try to make the system more efficient so that it can be executed perfectly every single time."

Companies that give The Celebrity Experience listen to their people. This is key! At the Gaylord, Danny is always asking the employees what they need to get the job done well. Is it extra time? People? Resources? Whatever it is, they get the tools they need. Hear this. You cannot expect your employees to give your customers The Celebrity Experience if they are working with bare-bones staff or resources. Instead of saving money, you are losing money because your team can't give your customers the kind of service that they will happily buzz about.

Recently, Danny worked with a test group of banquet service providers to reduce the time it took to serve a 2,000-plate dinner from three hours to one hour. "By listening to employees, we took procedures that used to take 20 steps and reduced them to 2 steps. When the trial period was completed, we announced to the test group that this would be the new process. They gave us a standing ovation. They said, 'Thank you for taking our suggestions and making our lives easier.' How do you think they then felt when they went out to serve the customer? They were elated, and that came through loud and clear."

Gather your employees and go through every detail of your customer's experience. Listen to their suggestions. They are the ones who know, and when they are involved in the process, they are more likely to buy into it. Take away anything that doesn't enhance your customer experience.

But remember, the magic isn't only in the details. Your systems are important, but your employees need to know when to relax the rules a bit. Traci Bild, a sales expert based in Tampa, Florida, told me of a time she visited a local coffeehouse. She was taking a little bit of time making up her mind about what she wanted to order. After a few moments, the young woman behind the counter said to her, "Would you hurry up? I've only got three minutes for each customer interaction, and you've used up two and a half minutes already." In this case, was the process enhancing the customer experience? Definitely not!

Once you have set your standard for your organization, and you provide constant and excellent training for your employees, then they will understand exactly what you expect of them. You'll also understand what you are looking for in an employee. If your brand is clearly defined, it will be easy to spot when your organization is not the right fit for an employee, and you can, and should, part ways. Even employees who don't have direct contact with customers must live up to your brand in order for you to give your customer The Celebrity Experience.

Celebrity Sighting

Corporate speaker and customer service expert Patricia Fripp relayed this story that was told to her by the president and owner of a coffee company, whom she met at the Young Presidents Organization (YPO) Family University held at the Ritz-Carlton in Atlanta. One particular time, he was on a ride-along with a driver who delivers coffee to the kitchen at the Ritz-Carlton. The kitchen staff at the Ritz thought that he was a delivery man. The man told Fripp, "It was hot and humid and I asked, 'Do you have a water fountain? I am very thirsty.' The kitchen worker left for a moment, and when he came back he had a beautiful blue Ritz-Carlton glass with water, ice, and a napkin and presented it with the same flourish as they would in a five-star restaurant." Says Fripp, "Now that is how you know if your core values and your customer service philosophy really work—when someone working in the kitchen, perceiving a thirsty delivery person, gives that kind of service. Customer service is not a department, it's not a slogan, it's an attitude that goes from top to bottom and across the board."

Take Three: Own Your Brand

A few years back I did some consulting for elder care corporations and their activities departments. As I visited several assisted-living centers, toured their communities, and read their brochures, I noticed that many had different names for the activities department. Some called it Community Life. Others, Resident Life. Still others, The Social Calendar. I also noticed something else. Their brands were all the same.

Take a look at their brochures, and it would tell you that your elderly parent would have choices like bingo, poker, craft classes, entertainment, theme days, and lunch bunch. If you were visiting three or four assisted-living communities to choose a place for your mom or dad or yourself to live, you were pretty much faced with the same activity choices no matter where you went. Nowadays there might be computer classes, exercise equipment, and a little Tai Chi thrown in. I'm not saying that the programs are bad. I'm just saying you can pretty much find the same activities everywhere you look. Unless you visit one of The Green House Project homes, such as Tabitha Senior Living, in Lincoln, Nebraska, or an assisted-living community that is registered with The Eden Alternative.

There you'll notice a difference. The plants. The animals. The children. Rarely are specific activities listed in their brochures; instead you'll find a statement about the way residents make their own choices about how they want to spend their days. Unless you went to Marian Manor in Virginia Beach, Virginia, where all the usual choices are offered, and the residents make and sell vintage wines, plan their own menus for dinner, and go crabbing in Chesapeake Bay every summer. Or unless your search took you to University Living in Ann Arbor, Michigan, where the elder residents take classes right alongside college students.

The difference between these communities and the rest is that they either own their brand or they have attached themselves to a very distinct brand (such as The Eden Alternative). While the others may have great activities and good programs, these resident life departments have a unique selling proposition. They own their brand.

Take a look at your competition. Look at their marketing materials. Look at their logos, their colors, their packaging, and their services. Now, be honest. Are yours really that different? Does your company stand out in a truly unique way? Or are you really just saying or doing more of the same in a different way?

Hub Plumbing & Mechanical in Boston, Massachusetts, owns its brand. There is no company like it in the area because it has differentiated itself in terms of service and overall look. I guarantee you won't find many plumbers, if any, who roll out red carpets to place their tools on.

When you think of coffeehouse, what brand comes to mind? Probably Starbucks. When you think fun airline? Southwest. Ice cream with a social conscience? Ben & Jerry's. These companies own their brands. There have been others that have tried to copy them, but they are the leaders in their industries.

What about you and your company? Are you the leaders? Are you copying what others do, or are others emulating you? Know this: People like to be affiliated with leaders. It makes them feel like they are in on what's cool and happening. It makes them feel like celebrities.

According to Karen Post, The Branding Diva, and author of *Brain Tattoos*, there are numerous ways you can differentiate your brand from your competitors' brands.

- Your credentials
- Your physical characteristics
- Your heritage

- Your size
- Your leadership in your industry
- Your expert team
- Your special ingredients
- Your speed of action
- Your personality
- Your style
- Your innovation
- Your technology
- Your pioneer status
- Your speed to market
- Your geographical location
- Your niche markets
- Your social consciousness
- Your environmental position

There are many more. Decide how your company is different from the competition and commit to living that difference every single day.

Take Four: Package and Promote

Once you become a customer of Hub Plumbing you realize you can trust them to deliver consistent, exceptional service. There's no doubt about it though, prior to the first encounter, what captures your attention are the red trucks, the red uniforms, and the red carpets bearing the company logo. They stand out from, say, another plumber in the Boston area, who drives around in a dirty, beat-up truck littered with coffee cups. Who do you want to trust your pipes to?

Like it or not, appearance matters. It's a fact Hollywood stars have known for years, and it's why they will spend millions on personal trainers, image consultants, hair and makeup artists, and designer clothes. They are building an image and a brand, and they know that the first thing their fans will notice about them is their appearance.

The same is true for your company. Consider every aspect of your company and how your look is or isn't true to your brand. Think about your dress code, marketing materials, building, vehicles, manuals, your web site, your invoices, your choice of signage. Are all of these areas consistent with your brand?

Don't forget employee-only areas either. Once, when I was speaking at a luxury hotel in Florida, I walked in through the employee break room. The walls were bland, the tables were dirty, the floor was scuffed, and it was just barren and dull all around. Once I walked into the lobby, which is seen by hotel guests, I was in a warm, clean, beautiful environment. Don't forget. If you want your employees to treat your customers like stars, then you need to model that by treating them like stars. If you want your employees to live up to your brand, then make sure they feel that brand everywhere—even in the places customers will never see.

Once you have a strong brand, make sure you put it out there so it is seen by your potential customers. Hub Plumbing is hard to miss because of its bright red trucks. However, owner John Wood is very intentional about getting the word out to his community. You'll read about Hub in local newspapers and hear John on the radio, and you might receive his monthly tips in your e-mail box. And you'll see those trucks, driven by Hub plumbers, in most of the city's annual parades.

Nido Qubein, president of High Point University, knows exactly how to toot the High Point horn. He watches for what he calls Kodak moments. When he noticed prospective students having their photos taken by their welcome signs in the parking circle, he had the signs redone so they bore the name, colors, and logo of the university. He did the same with the gorgeous fountain at the entrance and the statue of Atlas on the school's property. He saw where people were posing, and he placed the High Point signage or initials strategically so the name of the university would always be in the photograph.

Once you are clear about who you are, consistently live up to that standard, and strongly differentiate yourself from your competition, make sure that your look and feel is consistent with your brand, and then get the word out there about you and the fabulous red carpet treatment your customers receive.

Take Five: Encourage Personal Branding

Yes, you want everyone on your team to live and breathe your brand. Nevertheless, each person working for you comes to you with a unique style, personality, and gifts. Living the brand of your company does not have to mean squelching individual style. Consider the brand of Southwest Airlines. Casual, low-cost, and fun. Southwest employees are given specific uniforms and expected to have a sense of humor and be friendly with customers. How they express themselves within the context of that brand is up to them. Hence, you will fly on some flights where the attendants launch into elaborate comedy routines, and others where they are simply engaging without the high jinks. There is always room for individuality within your brand.

Wes Bard, president and CEO of Lutheran Home of Southbury, asks all of his employees to have their own personal mission statements. In fact, he uses it as a hiring tool. He discusses the mission of the company, and then asks his prospective employees what their mission is. If it's a mission that fits within that of the company, then he knows it's a good match. If it's not, then he suggests that the Lutheran Home may not be the place for them.

Ask each team member to consider what interests, gifts, or talents they might bring to your workplace that fit with the brand of the company, add to the customer experience, and ultimately brand them as individual people, too. For instance, in my travels I've met a tollbooth operator who gave out Tootsie Rolls, a singing server in a restaurant, a housekeeping supervisor who belly danced for customers, a bus driver who decorated his bus for every holiday, and a dog-loving banker who always had treats available for your pooch.

Set the standards that your employees must follow to ensure you're delivering a consistent customer experience. But let them know where there is leeway for individual touches and encourage your team members to express themselves as an extension of your brand.

Whatever your brand strategy, remember, ultimately, it's not about the uniforms, the logos, your web site, or what your brochures or commercials say. Your brand is defined by what your customers are saying about you. So know who you are, decide who you want to be. Be that consistently, and you'll soon be receiving branding ovations.

The Booger Principle

CELEBRITY EXPERT RITA TATEEL is a matchmaker for organizations that want to work with stars. The founder and president of The Celebrity Source, Inc., she keeps company with George Clooney, Jay Leno, Oprah Winfrey, Jack Nicholson, Harry Belafonte, and hundreds of Hollywood's best.

Based on her years of experience, here's what Rita had to tell me about celebrities:

One of the things I've discovered about celebrities is that they are some of the most insecure people on the planet. You see, when you're famous, you step outside your house and people recognize you and bend over backwards to be nice to you. As the celebrity, you don't know if what they are communicating to you is sincere or if they have an ulterior motive. You don't know if what they are saying is honest, or if they have a hidden agenda. You don't know who you should trust because people will take advantage of you if they figure they can because you represent power and influence. As a result, celebrities learn to mistrust people.

In order to gain their trust, Rita works hard to demonstrate that she is honest and will be forthcoming in every situation. She wants the celebrities she works with to know without a doubt that she truly cares about them and that she will take good care of them.

Sometimes that means being the bearer of bad news, and that takes courage.

One story Rita often tells is about the time she had contracted with a well-known movie star to be present at a special event. She had not yet met this celebrity but was told by others that he could be "difficult." Rita arranged to be at the entrance of the building, so that after the movie star walked the red carpet, she would be the first person he saw and she could escort him into the reception area. The star arrived and spent 30 minutes walking the red carpet with paparazzi taking his picture and fans screaming his name. When he arrived at the door, Rita went to shake his hand and she noticed that he had a very large, unsightly "something" hanging from his nose.

Everyone else had let that movie star pose for photos and walk the entire red carpet without even telling him he had a booger on his nose!

Rita took her hand, made a gesture under her own nose, and said "Do this." He followed suit, discovered the problem and took care of the embarrassing situation.

From that moment on, the so-called difficult celebrity was putty in her hands. Why? Because Rita cared enough about him to tell him something he needed to hear. She didn't try to pull one over on him, as the others did, and have a good laugh over it at his expense. No. She graciously and discreetly told him the truth, and as a result, he knew he could trust her.

Remember the old fable by Hans Christian Andersen about the emperor who had no clothes? Two crooks appear in the town pretending to be weavers. They enchant the vain emperor with their tale of having a magical weaving loom with which they can create beautiful clothes that are invisible to those who are dim and can't appreciate their beauty. He commissioned them to make him a robe, and when they were finished, he couldn't see it.

Rather than let others think he was so brainless and uncultured as to not be able to see the outfit, he went through the motions of putting it on and then paraded through the town so others could admire him in it. Of course, the townspeople didn't want their emperor to be angry with them, so they pretended to see the garment. It wasn't until a child shouted out the truth that "the emperor has no clothes" that others had the courage to admit that indeed their emperor was naked.

It takes courage to tell the emperor he has no clothes, but if you care about his well-being, then you will realize that sometimes it has to be done.

This brings us to The Booger Principle.

Have the Courage to Tell the Truth Because You Care!

Whether the others on the red carpet neglected to alert the movie star about his problem because they were being mean-spirited, or because they just thought they should ignore it, we'll never know. However, Rita knows that her job is to ensure that the celebrities she works with have everything they need to present themselves in the best possible light at each event. So, without knowing what the reaction of the celebrity would be, she told him what he needed to know . . . discreetly.

The Booger Principle, however, is about more than just this celebrity story. It's about those difficult conversations that we should be having with our customers, our employees, and ourselves. You know the ones I mean. The ones we avoid. Yet, it's important to have the courage to tell the truth because we care. When we don't, we are operating from a dishonest place, and our customers, our employees, and our businesses will ultimately pay the price.

Certainly celebrities pay the price when those who surround them refrain from telling them the truth. How often have we seen a young star continue spiraling down an unhealthy path because no one has the courage to be straight with her? In fact, The Booger Principle might be the one caveat to The Chicago Pizza Principle. Jo-Ann Geffen of JAG Entertainment told me, "What I find, very often, is that celebrities surround themselves, intentionally or not, with people who will just say 'Yes' to anything to keep the client happy. They do this instead of telling them what they really need to hear because they are afraid the celebrity will go elsewhere. If you have real integrity, you're going to care more about providing valid advice instead of simply appeasing them. I usually preface a relationship by saying 'Look, you don't have to accept what I'm telling you, but you're paying me so at least listen to my advice.'"

You'll notice that this chapter has a slightly different look from the other chapters. That's intentional. I don't have a model company to hold up as an example for you, and that's not surprising. The subject is an awkward one, and who wants to be known for having tough conversations with their customers and others? Instead, let's really take a look at The Booger Principle and get honest about why we avoid difficult discussions, which conversations we should be having, and how to best handle them.

Have the Courage

Picture this: You are a consultant who has been hired to help raise the morale and lower the turnover of an organization that is sinking. You are hired by the CEO to find out what the problem is and help fix it. You do your homework—assessments, surveys, focus groups, and intense conversations with both organizational employees and customers. The problem is clear, and it starts with the behavior of the CEO who signs your paychecks. What now? Do you tell him, or do you spend more time trying to find a different problem so you can avoid having the conversation?

You might be thinking, "Of course you tell him." You'd be right. However, it's easily said and not so easily done. Similar situations happened to two of my professional colleagues recently and, while they did the right thing, they had to draw from their own inner strength and courage to follow through. This is precisely why so many of these conversations that need to happen don't ever happen. They take courage. We avoid difficult conversations because we are afraid.

- We're afraid of the reaction from the person in question.
- We're afraid to upset our customer and perhaps lose his business.
- We're afraid to admit our own mistakes and perhaps lose business.
- We're afraid confronting the situation will bring up other issues we have to confront as well.
- We're afraid of putting ourselves and the other person in an uncomfortable position.
- We're afraid of hurting the other person's feelings.
- We're afraid we'll just be making the situation worse.

So, instead of dealing directly and honestly about the situation, we avoid the conversation and hope the problem will just disappear. Or, we talk to everyone else about the problem, behind the person's back, and hope that someone else will deal with it. Or, we pretend there is no problem and basically lie to our customers, employees, and ourselves by withholding the truth.

The problem with avoidance of these types of conversations is that there are costs involved. Depending on the specifics, there are costs to the customer, to the employee, and to you and your company. In the situation above, if the consultant isn't upfront with the CEO about the real source of his problems, the troubles the company is having will continue, and the consultant really hasn't done the job. It's an integrity issue. Could the consultant lose the customer? Possibly, if the CEO can't bear to take an honest look at himself. In the long run, the consultant will get more respect from customers, and from herself, if she deals with the problem head-on.

Other costs of avoiding conversations could include low morale, embarrassment, lack of growth, bottom-line losses when the truth comes out, or even something more serious. Having the courage to tell the truth and have those difficult conversations gives everyone the opportunity to grow, learn from mistakes, and avoid costly errors. You will honor yourself and your customers by finding the courage when you need it.

To Tell the Truth

At this point, you might be thinking about a few conversations you yourself have been avoiding. Or you might be asking yourself, "What are some of the situations that warrant having some kind of meaningful talk?" Certainly, if we just blurt out how we honestly feel about every customer or employee who is taking a bad day out on us, we might just find ourselves out of business. There are, however, situations where honesty is absolutely the best policy. Here are a few.

Tell the Truth When It's in Your Customer's Best Interest

Sam Horn, author of *Tongue Fu* and *POP! Stand Out in Any Crowd*, once told me a story about a big-name author who was being met at the airport by a 22-year-old woman employed by his publisher. They were to go together to a television studio to promote his book on a national program. When the big-name author arrived at the airport, he was drunk. The young woman knew that to allow him to proceed with the interview would be a disaster. So, despite his angry protests, she told him in no uncertain terms, "Sir, you are drunk, and I'm not going to allow you to go on this show." An author of his stature could have easily demanded that she lose her job, but she had courage and did what she felt was in the best interest of her customer. When the author sobered up, he was grateful, and now requests that he be escorted by this young woman to all media interviews.

No one likes to be the bearer of bad news, and sometimes it can feel easier to withhold information rather than tell your customers something they may not want to hear. This would be a lie. Put yourself in your customers' shoes. They are paying you for your expertise in whatever service or product you provide. While it may be easier to kowtow to your customers and avoid their potential anger, if you truly care about the people you serve you will tell them what they need to hear regardless of how they react.

Sometimes, the cost of avoiding difficult conversations is much greater than the potential embarrassment. In the next example, if the professional in question does not give her customers the complete truth it could cost them their lives or the lives of others.

Lory Smeltzer, CEO of Advanced Senior Solutions, a professional care management and life care planning company based in Clearwater, Florida, is faced with having critical conversations with her customers on a daily basis.

> When adult children of my elderly clients come to me, they are often in denial. They want and expect their parents to act as they did when they were in their 40s and 50s, and now Mom and Dad are in their 80s and 90s, and it's hard to watch that decline happen.
>
> The other day a daughter of one of my elder clients was visiting from out of town. I expressed concern to her about the fact that her father was still driving. He was on several medications for dementia-related illnesses, and had admitted to getting lost on several occasions. He was also hard of hearing and refused to wear his hearing aids. The daughter did not want to listen to me and responded by telling me, "He hasn't gotten into an accident yet." The man's son told me, "Oh, Dad's no worse than any other senior in his housing complex. They're all backing into one another!"

Sometimes the customers listen to Lory and sometimes, as in this case, they refuse to take her advice. Lory knows that in these instances she is running the risk of losing her customers because she isn't telling them what they want to hear. That's all right. "I just tell them, 'You've paid me to be your health care consultant. Do you want me to sugarcoat things and tell you what you want to hear? Or do you want me to give you the respect that you deserve and need, and tell you the truth?' Nine times out of ten they say, 'Tell me the truth, Lory.' And when they don't, at least I can sleep at night knowing that I did the right thing out of care for my clients."

When you are faced with a similar situation, put yourself in your customer's position. Wouldn't you want someone to tell you the truth? Tell them kindly. Tell them discreetly. But tell them.

Tell the Truth When Your Customer Isn't Right

Even when you are committed to making your customers feel like stars, you will find that sometimes you have to go against the old adage that "The customer is always right." Sometimes the customer is wrong.

As owner of Glickman Productions, an entertainment and event company, part of Bob Glickman's job is to cater to the wishes of celebrities performing at the functions he produces. Bob and his team will bend over backwards to make the celebrity feel comfortable, deliver on the requests of their contract rider, and generally be accommodating when they can. According to Bob, most celebrities are quite nice and very easy to work with.

However, occasionally, the celebrity will go too far. For instance, one starlet was scheduled to perform at 9:00 P.M. She approached Bob at 8:30 P.M. and said, "I'm tired. I'm just going to lie down and take a nap, and I'll let you know when I'm ready to go on." Says Bob, "We will go to almost any length to accommodate them, but there is only so far you can bend. I asked her to please prepare to go on or leave now and not get paid."

While the above example was that of someone not wanting to fulfill contractual obligations, we've all had experiences with customers who have been just as unreasonable. Giving your customers The Celebrity Experience does not mean tolerating behavior that is abusive toward employees and consistently and unreasonably demanding. Nor does it mean forever bending over backward for people who will clearly never be happy no matter how much you try to please them. Of course, you don't want you or your employees engaging in similar behavior by treating the customer poorly. However, there are certainly times when you need to take customers aside and let them know that they must respect your team members if they want to continue to do business with you. There are times when you must realize that you won't be able to satisfy these customers and must kindly suggest that a different company may have just what they are looking for.

Yes, sometimes it's best to compassionately, but firmly, fire your customer. Remember, in order for your employees to want to treat others like stars, they must feel like you treat them in the same manner. For most companies who give The Celebrity Experience this means putting your employees first. Which is worse? Losing the income from one customer or losing the respect and engagement of all of your employees?

Sometimes the customer is wrong, and you owe it to yourself, your team, and your company to tell them.

Tell the Truth When You've Made a Mistake

It's going to happen. If you are at a job or in business long enough, you're going to make mistakes. Or one or more of your team will make a mistake. It happens to the best of us. We are, after all, human. The key to staying true to providing exceptional customer experiences is to tell the truth about your mistakes and tell it quickly. Unfortunately, we live in a day and age where organizational blunders are denied, defended, swept under the rug, and blamed on other people and circumstances. This is absolutely the wrong approach if you honestly care about your customers and want them to trust you in the long run.

Instead, look to the example of David Neeleman, the founder and former CEO of JetBlue Airways. In early 2007, during an ice storm, the team at JetBlue made some decisions that kept an entire plane full of people stranded on the airplane at

JFK airport for 11 hours. During that time over 1,000 flights were cancelled, luggage was lost, and to say it was a debacle would be an understatement. While many CEOs would have defended their actions and placed blame on the circumstances, David Neeleman did no such thing. Instead, he took an action almost nonexistent in corporate America today. He apologized. He apologized, accepted blame for the fiasco, and took steps to ensure it would never happen again.

He spoke to his customers via the JetBlue blog and video. If you watched the video, you would have seen that he didn't give a terse statement read from a cue card, but a heartfelt admission of guilt, a promise to his customers, and a request for forgiveness. He embarked on a media tour, appearing on several news shows and late-night shows, and gave interviews for newspapers and magazines. He gave millions of dollars in refunds and vouchers and told his customers (and potential customers) exactly what actions had been taken to prevent this from ever happening again. A week later, when another ice storm hit, JetBlue had to cancel 400 flights due to FDA weather-related restrictions. The next day, David Neeleman posted a video on the JetBlue blog, updating customers on how the changes they had made, while not perfect, had enabled them to be up and running the next day.

Since that time, David Neeleman has resigned his position as CEO but remains with the company as Chairman of the Board. Regardless, the actions he took immediately following the failure began the process of rebuilding relationships with JetBlue customers.

As he has demonstrated, the key to regaining your customer's trust is to communicate, communicate, communicate . . . and communicate some more.

It starts by admitting to yourself that mistakes have been made. Remember, sometimes the emperor needs to be told he has no clothes. And sometimes the emperor is you.

Celebrity Sighting

Can you give people their memories back? Apparently, if you are Pam Huff or a member of the team at the Gaylord Opryland Resort and Convention Center, you can! Here's a story of a honeymoon gone wrong, and what the people at Gaylord like to call their "Memory Makeover."

Two guests arrived at the resort for their honeymoon. Unfortunately, mistakes were made on the part of the hotel staff, and the couple was so dissatisfied that they didn't even spend the night. Their wedding night had been ruined.

Because this situation fell short of Gaylord standards and wanting to make it right, the hotel management contacted the couple, apologized for the problems, and offered them a complimentary stay so they could experience what they should have experienced the first time. The new husband was very angry, though, and would have no part of it.

On their first anniversary his wife wanted to make him feel better about their botched honeymoon. She contacted the hotel and secretly took them up on the complimentary stay. She would surprise her husband with a second, and hopefully better, honeymoon.

This was a mission for Pam Huff and her Celebrity Services team. Pam questioned her team and they each had ideas to make this a special occasion. She took down their ideas and kept asking, "What else?" She wanted to make their stay as grand as possible. She questioned the wife about her wedding and looked at photos of the cake, the bouquet, and the bridesmaids' dresses. She and the wife discussed what they would have liked their honeymoon to have been like if mistakes hadn't been made.

On the day of the "Memory Makeover," Mrs. X convinced Mr. X to swing by the Gaylord on their way back from the movies because "there was a shop I wanted to stop in." When they arrived, the Celebrity Services team was waiting for them, complete with the red *carpet and a photographer to capture the new memories. The surprised husband was taken aback at first, but Pam explained that there was a special evening planned for him and his wife. His initial reluctance disappeared as their evening was revealed. The happy couple was escorted to their room—the Presidential Suite—where a beautiful wedding cake and a bottle of their favorite wine awaited them. The cake topper was an exact replica of the one they had for their wedding. There were rose petals on the bed and the bath, and candles everywhere. They were treated to dinner at the hotel's finest restaurant. The couple was floored.*

Even after they left, the surprises continued. Pam and her team piled in a limo about a week later. The "STAR Patrol" delivered balloons, homemade cookies, a framed photo of the two, and an album with photos from their second honeymoon to the newlyweds at their home.

The letter that the Gaylord team received from the husband said, "I now have to eat my own shoe because Pam made the impossible, possible, the unfixable, fixed. Pam and her staff gave my wife and me the only thing that really mattered—a memory." Now that's the way to handle your mistakes!

Tell the Truth about What You Can and Cannot Do

All right, I know what you're thinking. What about The Chicago Pizza Principle? Aren't we supposed to say "yes" to our customers and then figure out the how? Yes, I still believe that the foundation of giving your customers The Celebrity Experience is refusing to be satisfied with status quo and using your imagination to say yes to your customers whenever possible. There are, however, exceptions.

For instance, even Scott Graham at XPACS, which promises to deliver "anything and everything" won't do anything that isn't moral, ethical, or legal. You would not want to say yes to something that would endanger yourself, your employees, or your customer. You shouldn't say yes to something you know you won't follow through on. Don't make promises you aren't going to keep. Tell the truth about what you will and will not do. You shouldn't say yes to something if you simply don't have the expertise to deliver it. (Although you can partner with someone who does.)

For instance, when I was new in the speaking business, I accepted engagements from anyone and everyone who invited me to speak. However, I've long since learned that my expertise and speaking style are not right for every audience. Instead of taking a job in which I won't be able to give clients exactly what they need and expect from me, I will tell the truth and turn them down. Luckily, I have partnered with several other experts, and nine times out of ten I can recommend someone else who is perfect for the job.

Nothing is more frustrating to a customer than to be promised a bed of roses and receive a bed of thorns instead. Has a service technician ever promised he'd be at your house sometime this morning, only to show up at dinner time . . . the next day? Have you been promised the moon by your insurance company, only to find out what's not covered when you actually need to use it? Have you made a reservation for 6:00 P.M., only to arrive at the restaurant and be kept waiting until 6:25 P.M.?

It's better to be very clear about what you will and won't do, and what you can and cannot accomplish with your current resources. Then tell your customers the truth up front, and you will avoid their disappointment and anger when you don't deliver on your promises.

There are many other situations in which the truth is called for. You'll want to tell the truth when you aren't going to make your deadline, are double booked, are raising prices, or you don't have the answers to your problem. You'll want to tell the truth to your employees about what they may need to work on to become better service people or what's going on in the company. There's nothing that starts up the rumor mill more quickly than withholding critical information from your employees. Know this: If you don't give your employees the real story about changes or problems within your company, they will make up their own stories.

One hospital administrator shared with me that he and two other key leaders in his organization were all planning to retire within five years. In order to ensure there was an adequate succession plan in place, the administrator brought in a consultant who began to question employees about what they would look for in the new leadership. However, the administrator had neglected to alert his employees to the plan. The consultant wasn't in the building 30 minutes when the local newspaper called to say that an employee had contacted them with the news that leadership was being fired. The hospital was almost tomorrow's headlines because the administrator had failed to have an important conversation with his team.

In all of the situations mentioned, the best tactic is to communicate truthfully, quickly, and kindly. And it is the best tactic for you, too.

Because You Care

Telling the truth is about caring for the well-being of your customers, about earning and keeping their trust, and about giving yourself and your team opportunities to grow. Since the reason to have all those difficult conversations is that you care, it's important to handle them in a thoughtful manner. Here are a few tips to help you approach your Booger Principle discussions with careful compassion.

1. **Gather all the information.** Before you go into a conversation with a customer or employee, make sure that you have all of the facts you need.

   Sheri Riley is the president and founder of Glue, Inc., a company that works with corporations that have an entertainment component to their marketing. Once, Sheri was working with an actress whom she had on tour. There were many components to this tour, and many people were counting on this actress to be there for them. All of the details were set up so this actress knew exactly where she was supposed to be, when she was supposed to be there, what she was supposed to do, and with whom. However, she missed her flight. Sheri and her staff had been trying to get her to the right location all night yet the actress did not seem to be putting forth any effort on her end. When she finally arrived, they had to reassess everything. The radio sponsor was angry. The promoter was angry. Everyone who had spent money had lost some of it. To top it off, the actress didn't seem to want to participate in anything. She was snappy, rude, and disrespectful to everyone. She wanted to get out of doing the event when everyone else had been up for 24 hours rearranging and trying to make it happen on her behalf.

   Finally, Sheri decided to talk with her woman-to-woman. Everyone else had been running around trying to do things to appease her. Instead of doing the same, Sheri got in the limousine and simply asked her what was going on.

   It turns out that the actress had a major crisis happening with her teenage daughter. Her assistant, her makeup artist, and several of her entourage were all running around trying to work out the situation with her daughter, and she was here, in a silent panic.

"At that moment," says Sheri, "My assessment was, 'Wow! This problem is so much bigger than this event. Yes, people have lost money, and yes, this has been a challenging event, but this woman is dealing with a major emergency concerning her child!'"

Now that Sheri was connecting with her as a human being, she was able to empathize with the woman's situation. She asked her to carry out her contract for the rest of the day and then worked with her staff to get her on a plane home the same evening. She then arranged for the actress to complete her commitment at another time.

Remember, before you launch into a Booger Principle discussion, make sure you get all of the facts. This means you must ask questions and really listen. Give the other person or people involved an opportunity to share their side of the story. Only then can you make a fair decision about the next action that should be taken.

2. **Communicate quickly.** Once you have the facts, don't delay. Whether the situation in question involves the behavior of another or your own failings, the time to resolve it is now. Letting negative feelings fester because you want to avoid facing them is harmful to your employees and your customers. The more quickly you nip a problem in the bud (once you have all the facts), the more likely it will cease being a problem. Let it go on indefinitely and you may find you have a much bigger issue to contend with.

3. **Deliver the news in person.** In today's world, it's easy to hide, isn't it? Why walk over to someone's desk or call on the phone when you can simply fire off an e-mail? E-mail is a fantastic tool for delivering quick bites of information, asking questions, getting answers, and keeping up with friends.

However, it can be taken too far. I've seen arguments break out because someone misconstrued the tone of something communicated via e-mail. But, it's so easy. When you fire off an e-mail, you can just check that difficult discussion off your to-do list and you really don't even have to face it. Why, in 2006, Radio Shack fired 400 employees as part of planned budget cuts with one click of the send button. So, what's the problem?

The problem is that we are human beings and we deserve better. The problem is that when we refuse to face our problems head-on we cease to grow. The problem is that e-mail, while helpful in many ways, in situations like these, does not communicate that you care. And communicating that you care is the point of telling the truth.

4. **Put yourself in the other person's position and behave accordingly.** Consider how you would feel if you were in the other person's shoes. If you were the person in question, how would you want to receive this news? If this is a discussion you need to have with others in their best interests, or about their behavior, be discreet. Yelling at a customer or employee on the showroom floor is demeaning, regardless of the other person's antics. Pull the person aside and quietly and thoughtfully have your conversation. On the other hand, if you are the one who's in the wrong and you are in the position of having to apologize to your customers, lay it out there. JetBlue's David Neeleman used every available outlet to communicate his regret for the events that occurred during that ice storm. He did not defend the actions of his employees, nor did he place blame on any one person or group of persons. He *did* take full responsibility, and he did it loudly enough that everyone would hear. Were there consequences? Yes. But as we learned from the Enron fiasco, there are consequences either way. Your customers would rather you take the high road. Treat

each circumstance individually, and put yourself in the other person's shoes so you can decide how to best handle it.

5. **Be compassionate, but pull no punches.** You can be kind, gentle, and caring and still be honest. While you may be tempted to talk around a situation and hope the other party gets your meaning, this is not an effective way to tell the truth. Be very clear about what you need to say and say it. The sooner you honestly deal with the problem, the sooner it will be resolved and you can move on.

6. **Learn from Bob Hope.** Remember what comedy writer Gene Perret said about Bob Hope? "When I was in his presence, he made me feel important." This is the perfect time to practice that skill. Before you have your discussion, ask yourself, "How can I be absolutely honest with these people, and still ensure that they feel good about themselves when the conversation is finished?" You can do this by focusing on yourself and your feelings instead of firing off a list of everything they did wrong. You can do this by focusing on the behavior only, and not attacking people personally. You can do this by sincerely sharing what you do appreciate about them while you also ask for certain changes. Be kind, use gentle humor when appropriate, validate other people's feelings, and be clear about what needs to change and why. If you can communicate what needs to be said, affect change, and keep others feeling good about themselves, you'll know you have perfected the art of The Booger Principle.

When you have the courage to tell the truth because you care, you'll be building a relationship with your customers that has a foundation of trust. When trust is your foundation, even in the face of human error, you can still be known for giving a Celebrity Experience.

Be an A-List Customer

"You can provide really good theater, but if you don't teach them to be a good audience, people won't appreciate the effort."

—Dan Maddux, executive director of
the American Payroll Association

LET'S TALK ABOUT CELEBRITIES behaving badly. We've all heard tales of diva behavior from those who have allowed their stardom to go to their heads. They make all kinds of unreasonable demands, upsetting everyone in their wake.

Dan Maddux, the executive director of the American Payroll Association, knows all about difficult celebrities.

One well-known star whom Dan had hired to speak for his association's conference did an incredible show for the audience. However, behind the scenes she was not so charming. The staff of the APA had filled the dressing room with everything in her contract rider plus a bottle of her favorite wine and some beautiful flowers. She picked up the card and the flowers and stated, "I hate flowers . . . I hate to kill flowers." She continued to be unfriendly until it was time to have her picture taken, when she suddenly became "a love!"

Then there was the celebrity author who was "a total misery, bossing me around and belligerent. After about 30 minutes of this, he asked me, 'When am I going to meet the person in charge?'" Dan's answer? "You've been dumping on him for the last half an hour!" Dan, of course, was the person in charge.

Celebrity Dish

Henry Winkler, on the other hand, was wonderful. "When he spoke for the APA," says Dan, "he was so charming. When it came time for him to leave, my employee was going to escort him to the car. Instead, he walked out into the lobby and mingled with our members. I can't tell you the comments we got about that kind gesture! Perhaps that's why he's had such a long and fruitful career."

Awhile ago, I attended the red carpet arrivals of the *Pirates of the Caribbean: At World's End* world premiere. Some celebrities who walked the carpet, like Ricardo Antonio Chavira (of *Desperate Housewives*), Natalie Maines (of the Dixie Chicks), and Masi Oka (of *Heroes*) signed autographs and posed for fans who had cameras. Martin Landau was especially charming, clowning around and posing for every group of fans. Johnny Depp and Orlando Bloom smiled and waved as they made their way down the carpet.

On the other hand, there was the celebrity who did sign autographs, but visibly rolled his eyes every time a group of fans yelled his name to call him over. He posed for photos, but with a scowl on his face the entire time.

Yes, some celebrities behave badly and, if you keep up with

the news at all, you know that eye rolling and temper tantrums aren't even the half of it.

We love to dish about the diva side of some celebrities. Yet, as many customer service professionals will attest, the world of everyday people has its share of divas as well.

The Last Flight of the Night

Recently I took the last flight out of Denver, Colorado, headed for Florida. When I got to Atlanta, the last leg of my flight was canceled due to terrible weather. It was after midnight and I, along with everyone else, was exhausted. Now we had to stand in a long line at the airline reception desk trying to rearrange our plans and then find transportation to a local hotel.

Hey, it happens. It's just part of travel. I don't like it, but Mother Nature doesn't really ask for my opinions.

As I stood in the long line, inching my way to the reception desk, I couldn't believe the scene in front of me. A woman had collapsed toward the front of the line, and some of the airline staff members were pulled from the counter to assist her. Obviously, they needed to stay with her until an ambulance came.

Regardless, angry customers walked right past the scene, one by one, and harassed the poor service personnel behind the counter, who were now trying desperately to make up for the fact that two of their colleagues had been pulled out of commission. One man literally screamed at the people behind the counter for 20 full minutes, causing the rest of us to wait, and flustering the gentleman waiting on him. Did Mother Nature change her mind because he raised his voice? Nope. He still ended up in a hotel that night, just like everyone else in line.

When I finally made it to the counter, I smiled at the woman waiting on me and jokingly said, "I'll bet you're having a great night!" She laughed! Although I was exhausted, I tried to be patient as she checked flights and hotels for me. Then I thanked her for the all she was doing. Not only did I get on the earliest flight out the next morning, but my newfound friend put me in first class instead of coach!

Yes, this is the chapter where I turn the tables on the customer. You see, customer service goes both ways, and sometimes it is our own behavior that determines whether or not we receive The Celebrity Experience. If you want to receive red carpet customer service, you might want to take a real honest look at whether you are an A-list customer (someone customer service professionals look forward to serving) or a diva behaving badly.

A Cast of Real Characters

Here are some examples of just a few customers whom service people love to hate. Let's see if you've ever run across some of these characters in your travels.

"Chronic Complainer" Cathy. Cathy is the customer who is never happy. Service people groan when they see her coming because they know that no matter how much they bend over backward for her, she will still raise a fuss. She sends her food back multiple times, she moans about the price of various items, she whines about waiting for 10 minutes, she's either too hot or too cold, and, in short, she's just generally unhappy. If you tell Cathy about a special event happening on Monday, she wishes it were Tuesday. When you roll out the red carpet for Cathy, she goes on and on about how a blue carpet is so much nicer. You can bet that when Chronic Complainer Cathy shows up, service personnel are begging their coworkers to wait on her because they know it's a losing battle.

"Do You Know Who I Am?" Debbie. Debbie is under the impression that her needs take precedence over those of every other customer. She's the one cutting in front of the line "just for a second" or interrupting the server while he waits on another party. Debbie also believes that she is better than most of the people who serve her. She shows off her condescending attitude by snapping her fingers for service, rolling her eyes, making snide remarks, and over-enunciating her words because she thinks otherwise the server won't understand. She demands to be shown to her room at 12:00 P.M., even though check-in is at 3:00 P.M.; she demands extras with her meal that she is unwilling to pay for; and she generally demands special services not given to other customers, usually showing little to no appreciation when she gets them. And if you've made a mistake . . . well, beware. Do You Know Who I Am Debbie will be all over you, regardless of how often you apologize. While Debbie may occasionally get her way by bullying the staff, you can be sure that no one is bending over backward to give her The Celebrity Experience.

"Shoot the Messenger" Sam. Sam does not care that the human being in front of him does not control the weather, does not make the policies, does not set the prices, and does not cook the meal. Sam is unhappy because he's not getting his way, and he is going to take it out on the person who is convenient and available. Most of the time, this person is simply the messenger and has very little control over whether or not Sam's wishes are granted. Instead of kindly and respectfully asking for the person who might be able to help, he harasses, screams at, curses at, and can be outrageously rude to whomever is unfortunate enough to be in his path. Like the gentleman in my "Last Flight of the Night" story, Sam rarely gets his way, but he manages to make everyone within hearing range uncomfortable or downright miserable.

"I'm Too Busy to Be Bothered" Bob. Bob is the guy who is talking on his cell phone while he orders his coffee. His server must listen carefully and decide whether he is talking to the person on the other end of the phone or giving his order. He's the one who continues to talk to his companions in a restaurant while the waiter stands by the table waiting to be acknowledged. Bob is proud of his multitasking capabilities but rarely fully engages with the human being in front of him. He rarely makes eye contact, his smiles are cursory, and for all the attention he pays to the person who is serving him you'd think he was dealing with a robot. Bob could stand to take a few moments in his life to stop and smell the roses—or at least put his cell phone away temporarily.

"The Check's in the Mail" Charlie. Charlie might be charming. He might be funny. He might even be the friendliest guy in the room. His problem is, he doesn't want to pay. Charlie is the guy who eats in fancy restaurants but forgets his wallet at home. Or he brings just enough money for the meal, but not enough for a tip. Tip the hotel staff? Forget about it. He promises to pay for services in a timely manner, but it takes several phone calls and letters (or more) before he will send in the money he owes. And although he's reminded several times that policy is "payment on delivery," he has conveniently left his checkbook elsewhere when the goods arrive. Charlie may have good intentions but becomes known for making promises he just can't (or won't) keep.

Please don't misunderstand me. I believe that as customers we have the right to good service. If you've read this far, you know that I encourage service personnel to bend over backward and give outrageously fabulous service to their customers. I certainly believe that it is the job of service personnel to do whatever they can to make all customers feel as if they are the stars of the show.

I also believe that as a customer you have the right to complain if you are unhappy. You have the right to send your food back. To disagree with policies. To expect good service, and to speak up when you don't receive it.

Still.

Don't you think everyone deserves kindness and consideration, even when in disagreement? Anyone who has worked in service of the general public knows it is very difficult. On any given day, the service person will encounter one or, more than likely, more of the cast of characters listed above. Is it any wonder some of the best service people become cynical?

Even those who work with celebrities find that the most successful relationships are those with a boundary of mutual respect. Sheri Riley of Glue, Inc., told me she has a mantra she lives and works by.

When you respect yourself, then you can respect others. You really have to admire the talent of celebrities, while not elevating them above you or feeling that you are less than they are because their talents and their gifts are different. What that allows me to do is establish mutual respect from the get-go. We let every celebrity know that we have a boundary of both parties showing consideration for the other. When you set these boundaries, you've developed a solid foundation so that in providing customer service it does not come from a disrespectful place.

Being an A-list customer does not mean rolling over and accepting bad service. It does mean remembering that we are all human beings. We all have our human experience in common. Sometimes that means we make mistakes. Sometimes it means we have a bad day. Sometimes that means we can't be all that every person wants us to be. If you keep kindness as your top priority, even when you must find fault with the service you are receiving, you are well on your way to being an A-list customer.

Here are a few other action steps you can use to give those who serve you red carpet treatment.

Take One: Be Friendly

Take Two: Be Understanding

Take Three: Be Present

Take Four: Be Honorable

Take Five: Be Appreciative

Take One: Be Friendly

I asked Scott Graham of Xtreme Personal Assistant Concierge Services (of Chicago Pizza Principle fame) how he was able to get so much done through the power of his network. He responded, "It's all about the relationships we have with other people." When you have positive relationships with others, they will often bend over backward to help you.

Now please don't misunderstand. The reason to build relationships with those you do business with is not to be manipulative or to get special treatment. Rather, by making it a point to build those relationships, we'll have more fun, make new friends, and become known as someone others like to do business with. And, sometimes, people will bend over backward to help their friends.

Typically, you think about building relationships with work

colleagues or people in a networking group. However, what about your grocery store clerk? The waiter in your favorite restaurant? Your mailman? Your bank teller? Your electrician? I know the facilities director for a health care organization who makes it a point to become friendly with all of the vendors and suppliers he deals with. He does this because he enjoys having positive relationships with others, including the service people who assist him. As a result, he has received valuable tips from them, and some have even talked him through fixing something himself rather than hire them to do the job.

As you go about your day as a customer, consider making friends with the people with whom you do business. Get to know them. Say please and thank you. And be considerate of them and of other customers. The most well loved (and truly loved) celebrities are those who leave the Do You Know I Am? attitude at home and wait in line just like everyone else. And if you can wait in line with a smile on your face? Well, then you are really a star!

Take Two: Be Understanding

What does that bumper sticker say? Stuff Happens? Well, maybe those aren't the exact words, but you know the one I mean. People are going to make mistakes. The weather is going to cancel our plans. Sometimes we'll have to wait longer than other times. Sometimes the person serving us is having a horrible day. While we have every right to expect to be treated well when we are paying for goods and services, sometimes circumstances will occur that are beyond anyone's control—or at least beyond the control of the person in front of you. Yes, you have the right to complain, and in many instances it's the squeaky wheel that gets the grease. But as long as we're trotting out the old clichés, remember, you catch more flies with honey.

While you're at it, recognize that often the people delivering the message are *not* the people responsible for making the decisions. Give them a break. By all means, ask for the decision maker—but do so kindly.

Customers who understand that occasionally things won't go perfectly and still give everyone around them a smile and a positive word or two simply make the world a better place to live and do business in.

Take Three: Be Present

Have you ever carried on a complete transaction with a service person and never shared eye contact or exchanged smiles. Sure. We all have. Sometimes the lack of engagement is on the part of the service person who is bored, watching the time clock, or gossiping with a colleague while ringing up your purchases. Sometimes, however, it's on the part of the customer, who is lost in thought, in a rush to move on to the next appointment, gabbing with friends, or carrying on a cell phone conversation while making purchases. What we don't realize when we are doing all this multitasking is that the transaction actually takes longer. The server is waiting to get your attention, you've got to repeat what's already been said, and mistakes are easily made.

Sometimes the way to get others to engage with us is to engage with them. A friendly hello. A smile. Eye contact. Using a name. Dave Timmons, of Six String Leadership, taught me to use the name of the person serving me. Sometimes I'll go through an entire transaction at a grocery store, and the person ringing up my purchases doesn't look at me once. When the transaction is done, I'll say, "thank-you" and add the person's name at the end. Nine times out of ten, I get eye contact and a smile for the first time. Perhaps Dale Carnegie was right. There *is* no sweeter sound than that of your own name.

If we want those serving us to remember that we are living, breathing human beings, and not numbers, then we must be willing to give them the same respect and attention. This means not carrying on cell phone conversations while ordering coffee at Starbucks, and temporarily ending the conversation with your friends to pay attention to the waiter who is neglecting other customers while he stands by and waits for you to acknowledge him.

You can do your part to make each customer service exchange more efficient, more pleasant, and more likely to result in red carpet service.

Take Four: Be Honorable

Pay your bills. Be respectful of the property of others. Remember that the hotel towels belong to the hotel—unless you purchase them. Tip your waiter, your bell person, your baggage checker, and others who rely on your tips to earn a living. Use the 13-item or fewer aisles only if you have 13 items or fewer. Keep your comments appropriate, and make no assumptions about the person serving you. Be trustworthy and honorable, and you'll be the kind of customer it's a pleasure to serve.

Take Five: Be Appreciative

The facilities director of a health care company, whom I wrote of earlier, told me of the time he had a problem with the telephone company. He was feeling stressed because he anticipated dealing with the problem for several days, having to make repeated phone calls and write repeated letters. Instead, the problem was fixed within 24 hours. So he picked up the phone and called a representative at the phone company and thanked her. First, on the other end of the phone, there was stunned silence.

Then he was asked to hold. The phone company rep came back, put him on speaker phone, and asked him to repeat what he had just said for the five other people she had brought into the room. She told him that in all of her years working for the phone company she had *never* received a thank-you call. It tickled her so much she had to share it with her coworkers, who were equally amazed.

Isn't that the way? We are often so quick to complain, but when service is great we don't always take the time to say thank-you! I guess it's just human nature.

Being an A-list customer means taking the time to find the manager and letting that person know what a fantastic job the employee did serving you today. It means filling out comment cards and the surveys that are sent to you after your customer experience. It means sending a letter of praise about a specific employee after you've been wowed by the customer service that has been delivered. Oftentimes, promotions, pay raises, and awards are given based on the feedback from customers. If people have provided you with a fabulous experience, wouldn't you want them to be rewarded?

Even if you have constructive criticism, filling out comment cards is appreciated by the team. Ensure that your criticism is constructive, though. Be specific in the changes you'd like to see. General comments (or heaven forbid, mean-spirited comments) aren't helpful and really serve no purpose except, perhaps, to give the writer an opportunity to vent. Be specific with your criticisms, and you may find the leaders of the establishment have learned from them.

However, if you find that you fill out comment cards or speak up only when you have a criticism to share, you might want to balance that out with appreciative comments. If people have made your day with their exceptional service, why not make theirs?

Let me end this chapter by reiterating that I believe that when we are paying for services, we deserve to receive the best customer service the establishment has to offer. This is not about rolling over and passively accepting poor service. As a matter of fact, I believe we do too much of this already and should begin to expect good customer service if not great customer service. However, we must admit that sometimes the behavior of certain customers points more toward their being divas than A-list customers. Think about how you might contribute to a positive customer experience by being a positive customer. At the very least, you'll improve your day and the days of others you come in contact with. You might also just find that more and more you begin to receive The Celebrity Experience!

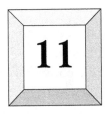

That's a Wrap!

IMAGINE A WORLD where you had a job that fueled your passion, used your creativity, and kept you energized and constantly thinking about how you could top yourself.

Imagine a business where the team of people you worked with were full of excitement and enthusiasm, falling all over themselves to talk about their ideas for really wowing your customers . . . and then some.

Imagine a scenario where your customers were blown away with the lengths to which you have gone to make them feel special, where they give you their loyalty, where they spend more money, and where they tell anyone who will listen about how you have made them feel as fabulous as a Hollywood star.

Imagine . . .

That's exactly what the members of our Celebrity Experience Hall of Fame did before they made the decision to give their customers red carpet treatment.

The leaders at Tabitha Health Care Services imagined what it would be like to say "yes" to the dreams of their residents and create a culture of total innovation.

The forward thinkers at High Point University imagined what it would be like to create an extraordinary experience for their students, faculty, staff, and alumni.

Pam Huff and her team at the Gaylord Opryland Resort and Convention Center Celebrity Services Department (along with the other Gaylord Celebrity Service departments) imagined what it meant to give meeting planners and others the star treatment.

Dave Timmons of Six String Leadership, Inc. imagined what it would look like if he paid attention to that which grips the heart of the people in front of him and used that information in unique ways to make them feel special.

Dan Maddux of The American Payroll Association imagined how the APA could shine the spotlight on professionals who have never been given much applause, and create a culture of much-deserved standing ovations.

The founders of NASCAR imagined a sports entertainment venue where the fan was at the forefront and the celebrities were accessible.

John Wood of Hub Plumbing & Mechanical, Inc. imagined what it would look like if he raised the standard of service in his profession and literally rolled out the red carpet for his customers.

Gena Pitts of Professional Sports Wives imagined a world where the person who always stands to the side of the celebrity spouse had a place to go where others who understood could be supportive.

And the founding team at Jobing.com imagined a company culture that was unlike any other company, and where employees, who were treated like royalty, would in turn treat customers like stars.

Now that you've read their stories, as well as the stories of those who serve celebrity clientele, you may be imagining several ways that you can bring The Celebrity Experience to life in your business.

Fabulous!

The next step is to make the decision that each of the Celebrity Experience providers above made from the beginning.

The decision to say, "yes!"

Yes! To delivering extraordinary red carpet customer service . . . and then some.

Yes! To leading a team of people who are excited about the work they do.

Yes! To creating a culture where employees and customers are stars.

Once you say yes, and really commit to your decision, all other decisions you make in the future will stem from that one.

In my mind, it is The Chicago Pizza Principle that lays the foundation for every single strategy set forth in this book. You must have the same kind of Yes! attitude that Scott Graham and his team have if you are going to give your customers a genuine Celebrity Experience.

Not no, not maybe, not I think so or probably . . . but an un-equivocal yes! Yes, we want to do this, we can do this, and we will do this!

It is this attitude that separates the people who make great things happen in their organizations from those who don't.

Once you've made the decision to say yes, then the question is, "How?"

I imagine the answer will be different for every person and

every organization. However, here are a few steps to get you started:

Step One: Own Up

Answer the question, "Where are we now?" How do your customers and employees currently feel about your company? What are they saying when they talk about your organization? How often are they availing themselves of your services? How much of your business comes from repeat customers? How much money are your customers spending with your company? Are you meeting your financial goals? Every month?

Survey your customers and employees—formally and informally. Go out on the floor and watch the customer interactions. Hire a secret shopper. Remember, do this with the attitude of looking for ways of improving your customer service—not with an eye toward judging and reprimanding your employees. This is simply to gather information.

Get together with some team members, get really honest with yourselves, and answer the following questions:

- Where are we saying no to our customers when we could be saying yes?
- What kind of first impression are we making on our customers?
- How well do we really know our customers?
- Are we using that information in unique ways to make them feel special?
- Have we created a place where our customers have a sense of belonging?
- Have we created a place where our customers feel like they can have whatever they want?
- And then some?
- In what ways do we give power to our customers?

- Do we have a clear-cut brand?
- Are we honestly living up to what it says on our brochure and marketing materials every single day?
- Do we treat all customers as though they deserve exceptional customer service or just the big spenders?
- Do we treat our employees the way we want them to treat our customers?
- How are the results we are seeing (or not seeing) a reflection of how we treat our employees?
- Are we having the conversations we should be having with our customers?
- With our employees?
- With ourselves?
- Do we have the "cast" we need to put on an award-winning "show"?
- Are we willing to do what it takes to become a Celebrity Experience provider?

Step Two: Dream Big

This is the step where you gather your team together and let them in on what you've been learning about delivering red carpet customer service. If you like, give them a copy of this book, and ask them to come together after you've all read it. Or simply tell them how and why you were inspired by The Celebrity Experience. Then, invite them to dream with you. Remember, the more you involve the entire team in creating the vision for your company, the more likely they will buy into it.

Here are a few key questions to get the brainstorming started.

- If Johnny Depp or Meryl Streep were to walk into our place of business right now, how would we treat them differently from the way we treat our other customers?

- What would it look like if we were able to give our customers whatever they asked for? (Thank you, Maria Motsavage of Ideal Senior Living, for this question.)
- What could red carpet customer service look like for our company?
- What could red carpet customer service look like in our department?
- In your wildest dreams, what would you like to provide for your customers and employees?

Once you've got a variety of answers to these questions, and everyone's input, craft a clear-cut, compelling vision that will get everyone excited, jumping in, and moving forward with the plans. Remember what I wrote earlier? One of the strategies that each of the celebrity service companies and the members of the Celebrity Experience Hall of Fame employed was to create the vision and talk about it—to every employee—every single day. Make it simple, easy to understand, and something you will be excited about communicating on a daily basis. Find as many ways as you can to bring your vision to life for your employees. Have elaborate launch parties, write about it in your newsletter, put it on the employee web site, give each employee a reminder card to carry around, write songs about it, and create a humorous video about your vision to show your team. Better yet, get them to create the video.

Step Three: Decide on Tangible Results

Make sure that you and your team know how you will know if you've succeeded in your quest. Deciding on tangible results to strive for will let you know if you're on track with your efforts.

- What concrete, measurable results are you shooting for?
- What will customers think, feel, or say about your business?

- What will your customers do differently as a result of your efforts?
- How much money will your customers spend with your organization?
- How many letters of appreciation will you receive?
- How many referrals will your customers give you?
- How will employee turnover change as a result of your customer service efforts?
- Will you receive media attention?
- Will you be named a member of The Celebrity Experience Hall of Fame?
- Will you be highlighted in Donna Cutting's next book?

Step Four: Strategize and Prioritize

Technically, that's two steps, but I believe they go together. Once you have a strong vision of where you'd like to be and a clear idea of what it will look like once you get there, it's time to decide on the action steps you'll take to get there. These can be large or small. They can come from ideas you read in this book, they can come from the creative minds of you and your team, or they can come from both. These are the things you will do to begin making your customers feel like stars.

List them.

When Nido Qubein took on the role of president of High Point University, he and his team listed almost 200 strategies that they would employ in pursuit of their vision of being extraordinary. Some of them were simple, such as having a gumball machine in the president's office or putting welcome signs out for visitors. Others were more complicated, such as beginning an extensive renovation project.

What are your strategies? List what you will do as a company, as a department, as an individual to move toward your goal of delivering The Celebrity Experience to your customers.

Once you've strategized, prioritize. What will you do first? Next? Next? What simple items can you do immediately? What will take more planning and money?

WARNING: This is where most individuals/teams stop. Do not stay on this step forever. Planning is important, but while many teams are having meeting after meeting after meeting to plan what they intend to do, providers of The Celebrity Experience know that strategizing and prioritizing is an ongoing process. They know that you can't really know how it's all going to turn out until you start doing.

Remember, a movie isn't really a movie until the director says, "action!"

Step Five: Take Action!

Go for it! Look at your list of strategies and start trying them out. You can always adjust, and you will, but you won't know how something is going to work until you try it.

- Buy the red carpet.
- Roll it out.
- Do the "Chicken Soup" exercise.
- Remember something unique about a customer and refer to it the next time.
- Set out a welcome sign for your next appointment.
- Say yes to a customer and then figure out how.
- Give your customers swag.

- Give your customers a choice.
- Give back to the community.
- Notice the great job your employees or co-workers are doing and tell them.
- Do what needs to be done to live up to the descriptions on your marketing materials.

Whatever your strategies are, implement them. You can try them out first. Be like Kevin Spivey, director of housekeeping at the Gaylord Opryland, who went into the lobby and began by showing guests the way to their rooms, and then challenged his team to do the same. Action spurs action, and once you take action, your strategies and plans will take on a life of their own.

Step Six: Review and Edit

Once you've started, you can then go back and reevaluate.

- What's working?
- What's not working?
- Is what we're doing adding to the customer's experience?
- What systems do we need to put into place to make this particular strategy part of our everyday routine?
- Are our efforts producing the results we have hoped for?
- Is everyone in our cast committed to our vision?

When you have the answers to these questions, you will know which strategies to keep, which ones to change, and which ones to drop altogether. Do not, however, let the fact that a strategy is difficult to implement keep you from doing so if it truly enhances your customer's experience. Remember, that's the difference between Celebrity Experience providers and others. If it's a winning idea, you simply need to find a system that makes it easy to implement. Scale back if you must, but choose your customer over convenience.

Step Seven: Celebrate

The Oscars wouldn't be the Oscars without the after-parties, right? As you continue on your journey toward being a Celebrity Experience provider, be sure to celebrate along the way. Reward your employees for the fan mail they receive from your customers. Give standing ovations for every success. Invite your customers to party along with you!

Celebrate and continue the journey.

As I bring this book to a close, I am reminded of something Irene Cara told me. Irene is an actress and musician who received an Academy Award, two Grammy Awards, a Golden Globe, and a People's Choice award in 1983 for cowriting and performing the song, "What a Feeling" from the movie *Flashdance*.

Prior to that year, in 1980, she performed two songs—"Fame" and "Out There on My Own"—both nominated songs from the movie *Fame*, at the Academy Awards ceremony.

She said, "There I was, just 20 years old, and new to the business. I was standing backstage getting ready to go on, and I was terrified. I glanced over to one side and there was the great actress Mary Tyler Moore, waiting in the wings to present an award. And *she* looked nervous! Down the hall was living legend Gene Kelly who was to perform a dance on stage soon. And *his* palms were sweaty! I couldn't get over that after all of their years in this business, they had just as many butterflies as I did and were just as excited as I was—the new kid on the block."

And so it is when you choose to say yes to greatness. You never settle or get complacent. Your biggest challenge becomes how to top yourself. You are constantly asking, "What's next?" As a result, you get to join the ranks of people like Scott Graham, Pam Huff, John Wood, Nido Qubein, and the others who bring zeal to their work that is unsurpassed. It's what gives them and their organizations star quality.

It is with this knowledge that I invite you to tap into your own star quality, roll out that red carpet, and give your customers The Celebrity Experience.

Resources

MANY OF THE CELEBRITY service companies and celebrities high-lighted in this book also serve corporate clients. Here is their contact information:

Xtreme Personal Assistant Concierge Services (XPACS)
2901 W. Coast Highway, Suite 200
Newport Beach, CA 92663
949-258-4389
www.goxpacs.com

The Celebrity Source
8033 Sunset Blvd., #2500
Los Angeles, CA 90046
323-651-3300
www.celebritysource.com

The Campins Company
605 Lincoln Road, Suite 300
Miami Beach, FL 33139
305-531-2277
www.TheCampinsCompany.com
www.TCCSE.com

Marquis Jet
230 Park Avenue, Suite 840
New York, NY 10169
212-499-3790
www.MarquisJet.com

The Jack Canfield Companies
World Headquarters
P.O. Box 30880
Santa Barbara, CA 93130
805-563-2935
www.jackcanfield.com

Gene Perret
http://members.aol.com/geneperret/

JAG Entertainment
4265 Hazeltine Ave.
Sherman Oaks, CA 91423
818-905-5511
www.jagpr.com

Glue, Inc.
www.glueinc.com

Members of the Celebrity Experience Hall of Fame

Tabitha Health Care Services
4720 Randolph Street
Lincoln, NE 68510
402-486-8520
www.tabitha.org

High Point University
833 Montlieu Avenue
High Point, NC 27262
800-345-6993
www.highpoint.edu

Gaylord Opryland Resort and Convention Center
2800 Opryland Drive
Nashville, TN 37214-1297
615-889-1000
www.gaylordhotels.com

Six String Leadership, Inc.
P.O. Box 340025
Tampa, FL 33694-0025
813-948-6709
www.davetimmons.com

American Payroll Association
San Antonio Office
660 North Main Ave., Suite 100
San Antonio, TX 78205-1217
210-226-4600
www.americanpayroll.org

NASCAR
866-722-5299
www.NASCAR.com

Hub Plumbing & Mechanical
1444 Dorchester Avenue
Boston, MA 02205
866-482-7586
www.hubplumbing.com

The Professional Sports Wives Association, Inc.
The Terrace at Windward
3070 Windward Plaza, Suite F-352
Alpharetta, GA 30005
www.prosportswives.com

Jobing.com
Phoenix Office
4747 North 22nd Street, Suite 100
Phoenix, AZ 85016
602-200-6800
www.jobing.com

Bibliography

Post, Karen. 2002. "In A Sea of Sameness, Brands Must Stand Out." *Brain Tattoo*, Issue 1. http://www.brandingdiva.com.

Promotional Products Association International. 2004. "Promotional Products: Impact, Exposure And Influence: A Survey of Business Travelers at DFW Airport." http://www.ppa.org (accessed April 29, 2007).

About the Author

DONNA CUTTING IS A RECOGNIZED EXPERT in employee morale, recognition, and personalized customer service. Corporations, associations, and others call upon Donna regularly to give presentations that help leaders create workplaces where employees get standing ovations and customers have a Celebrity Experience.

No ordinary speaker, Donna draws on her experience as an actress and her passion for fun, and delivers her content with her trademark enthusiasm and theatrical style. She's known for her Keynote Theater presentations, through which she truly gives her audience members a Celebrity Experience by making them the stars of her show. Donna combines her humorous and dramatic style of speaking with easy and action-oriented, practical ideas and strategies that can be implemented immediately.

She spent the first half of her career working as an elder care professional and consultant. Today, she speaks for and trains professionals who work in elder care, health care, finance, hospitality, education, and human resources as well as other fields. Through her research with people who serve celebrities she developed The Celebrity Experience.

215

Donna is a member of the National Speakers Association and is a past president of the National Speakers Association of Central Florida.

She lives in St. Petersburg, Florida, with her husband, Jim, and their Maltese puppy, Snowball. One of her dreams is to walk the red carpet and attend the Academy Awards, which she watches on television, without fail, every single year.

You can reach Donna at:

Donna Cutting Presents
P.O. Box 76461
St. Petersburg, FL 33734
Phone: 727-525-5818
E-mail: donna@donnacutting.com
Web site: www.thecelebrityexperience.com

Do you or your company belong in

The Celebrity Experience Hall of Fame?

Have you been inspired by *The Celebrity Experience* and taken action on the ideas presented in the book? Do you think your company belongs in The Celebrity Experience Hall of Fame? Do you know an individual who really rolls out the red carpet for customers? Someone who deserves a little red carpet treatment himself?

Contact Donna and let her know that you are interested in submitting an entry for:

The Celebrity Experience Hall of Fame

In 2008, in what we hope will be an annual competition, we will select one company or organization and one individual to become members of The Celebrity Experience Hall of Fame. Leaders from the selected company or organization and the selected individual will receive prizes that constitute the red carpet treatment and will be featured in Donna's next book in *The Celebrity Experience* series. Runners-up will also be featured in the next book. Interested? Contact Donna for official rules, prizes, and information.

Donna Cutting Presents
Attention: Celebrity Experience Hall of Fame
P.O. Box 76461
St. Petersburg, FL 33734

or

CelebrityExperienceContest@DonnaCutting.com

A percentage of the author's royalties from
The Celebrity Experience will be donated to
Second Wind Dreams.

Second Wind Dreams

Second Wind Dreams is a national non-profit organization with the goal of bringing seniors to the forefront of our society by enriching their lives and empowering them to age with dignity. It accomplishes this goal by fulfilling the dreams of those living in elder care communities.

Like Donna Cutting, the people at Second Wind Dreams know that you are never too old to dream.

Second Wind Dreams
1031 Cambridge Sq., Suite G
Alpharetta, GA 30004
678-624-0500
www.secondwind.org

Index